What's in the Water?

What's in the Water?

Our Soul's Reflection on Spirit and Self

Mike Russell

What's in the Water?
Our Soul's Reflection on Spirit and Self

Copyright © 2020 by Mike Russell

All rights reserved. No part of this book may be used or reproduced by any means, graphic, electronic, or mechanical, including photocopying, recording, taping, or by any information storage retrieval system without the written permission of the publisher except in the case of brief quotations embodied in critical articles and reviews.

ISBN: 978-1-7330393-1-4
ISBN: 1-7330393-1-7
Library of Congress Control Number: 2020915561

Sacred Life Publishers™
SacredLife.com
Printed in the United States of America

DEDICATION

There are times in one's life that time stands still, and extraordinary events happen that cause a trajectory change. No longer in the box that humanity places around us with the conditions imposed by people, these events whether good or bad impose a wake-up call which invites us to pay attention. My own wake-up call came in form of the spiritual door opening after the death of someone I loved. There was no turning back for me as I could not put the genie back in the bottle, nor would I want to.

I would like to dedicate this book to all of you that seek to know yourself and your relationship to whatever you believe in. You are the pioneers of heart and will add your newfound knowledge to the winds of change as the world wakes up to the possibilities of the future. May your journey be meaningful to you and give you the peace of under-standing that you are the pivotal center of this new energy field.

CONTENTS

Dedication v
Introduction xi

Chapter 1 - SPIRITUAL

Starbucks Spirituality 1
My Father's Hands 3
Walk Away 4
Walk in My Shoes 6
    Poem – *Flash of Time* 8
You Don't Know What It Feels Like to Be in Someone Else's
    Shoes Unless You Wear Them 10
What Is in a Birthday? 12
    Poem – *To Remember* 15
Look Closer 16
How Great Thou Art 18
Beneath the Surface 20
    Poem – *Stand Tall* 22
Our Amnesia to Spirit 23
A Rainbow in the Storm 25
The Miracle of Now 27
The Spiritual Dandelion 29
    Poem – *Coming to the Center* 32
The Wear Marks of Life 34

The Still, Small Voice 35
In the Eyes of Spirit 37
Wanting a Spiritual Experience 40
    Poem – *The Birth* 43
The Soul's Journey 45
My Way Is the Best Way 47
Controlling Faith 48
Seeing Stars 50
When Does Life Really Begin? 53
Green-Eyed Lady 55
    Poem – *Synchronicity* 58

Chapter 2 – FEAR

Let Spirit Bring You Home 59
Being Okay Now 63
    Poem – *Stepping Into the Light* 66
Life Lessons 68
Miffdom 69
The Jump Rope of My Life 71
I Am on Your Team 74
    Poem – *To Know* 77
The Thread of Love 78
My Reasons for Being Here 79
Faith 82
Resetting the Grandfather Clock 85
Acceptance 87

Chapter 3 – RISK

The Bird Party 91
I Am the Angel, You Are the Angel 92
The Hand of God 94
The Case of Being Naïve 96
Freefalling into a New Story 99
One Hand to Another 101
Floating Down the River of Life 103
Reaching Out to Risk 105
Midlife to Cool 107
Skating to Freedom 108
Hanging Out in Life 109
Jack's Passion 111
Look up and Change Your Conditioning 114
The Hallelujah Experience 115

Chapter 4 – EGO

The Basics Are Good Enough 119
Seeing Differently 120
A Lesson from the Child on The Roof 122
Held by the Confines of Ego 124
Around Sound 126
Sending Guilt Packing 127
Raccoon Metaphor 130

Poem – Why? 133
Let the Guitar Sleep 134
Things Happen 137

Chapter 5 – GRIEF/FORGIVING

Leaves on the Forest Floor 139
    Poem – *Talk to the Wind* 143
Lessons Learned 144
The Planned Journey 147
Seen It All 149
Saying Good-bye 151
The Three Points 156
    Poem – *Separation* 161
A Short Walk to Forgiveness 162
Dropping into Memory 164
New Beginnings 166
A More Peaceful Definition 168
Boxed In 170
    Poem – *Peace* 173
Transitions 174
The Ring 175
    Poem – *All Is Well* 179
Acknowledgments 181
About the Author 183

INTRODUCTION

Many years ago, in a land far away—I've always wanted to say that—I was conceived by what I now know was an agreement among myself, my English mother, and my American father serving in the Air Force. I assume I was wanted, and it is staying that way because I never asked them and can't now that they are gone.

I realized very early in life that I was put on this earth to drive my older brother crazy. I was faster and stronger and could yell like a banshee when the time was right to get him into trouble because my poor parents, looking at my innocent face, would never have suspected that no matter what that my brother wasn't to blame in some fashion. My brother is not here either, so my memories are the ones that will always color the story of a child that regularly sensed that something was going on in this universe involving a deeper meaning, not just a random act of kindness by an unseen force.

Growing up in many churches while my family moved with each of my father's air force deployments gave me the opportunity to see and compare the different religions around the world. Although they are the same in some capacity, all these churches proved to me that none of them had "the answer," not that a child necessarily knows what the question is. But I did know that there was more to life than following a set of rules that seemed to change based on which church we were in at the time, giving money to building its funds, and decided that I only liked a church if the minister had a sense of humor. My reasoning was that humor had to be something given to us as a gift to offset all the pain and suffering I had the honor of seeing in different places that my father was stationed.

In my youth, I graded the church on whether a minister could make me laugh, which I took as a sign that I should pay attention. Rationality is not necessarily part of a kid's life and seemed to be just as important as all the adults' concerns and frustrations about building a church. After all, I was always watching my parents and others focusing on the dos and don'ts of a church, and I never sensed that they were having fun, just going through the process of churchliness. I know that is probably not true, but that is what I saw.

So, the result of attending so many churches while growing up allowed me to lump all of them into one, which turned out to be an advantage in a way. I learned early that dogma was pretty much the same wherever I went, and I put it on the lowest shelf of my church life. To me, church was a social place where I got to hang out with friends, learn to like girls, go to camps, start to understand group dynamics, and generally see that, no matter where we traveled, people were the same everywhere. Skin color, language, and other facets of life might change, but generally, people around the world had the same wants and needs and drank the same water that I did.

This realization began a lifetime of my trying to comprehend my own acceptance and understanding of why I am here, what I needed to learn, and what that meant for me because I knew I was heading somewhere different than where I was. We all do this whether we talk about it or not. During my ensuing school years, getting married, having children, and all the things that go with that, which intervene and dilute the big question, it keeps the trajectory the same. We are all headed somewhere no matter what you believe. Whether I chose to focus on my journey or whether I went with the storyline of what was happening at a point in time, it never took away from the challenge of trying to understand the real questions I always had about my connection to Spirit and all the sub questions related to that one.

Not until my wife Barbara died and I suddenly found myself facing mortality did all those questions I had all my life come bubbling to the surface. The door opened widely, and being a firm believer in options, I chose to walk through that door and open my world to Spirit, as I understand it, and try to answer some of the questions within the confines of the rest of my life. It has been an up-and-down journey with no regrets.

On this journey I have had the privilege of writing about things that have happened to me along the way and what they mean to me. I can't say that by reading this book, readers will have spiritual insight of their own. I can only tell readers that I am what I consider to be a normal person, affected by things that have happened since my childhood, and thanks to my connection to new friends in the Angelic realm, friends on the same journey, and my partnership with my second wife, Trisha Michael, I am in a position to be able to write my thoughts down and share along the way. This compilation will hopefully give you a fun way to see a journey that we can all have and apply it to your own experiences. There is no right or wrong in the Spirit world, as I am often told, so what you take with you is good and perfect. I want to just invite you along with me as I apply what I hear, see, feel, and know and try to figure out where the puzzle pieces fit together.

When we were traveling around the world, my mother used to say, "What's in the water?" In some cases I didn't really want to know what was in that water, but the journey to find some meaning behind the water's flow as we travel from being born to going home is a trip that I am happy to be on, and I look forward to seeing where I can dock my raft.

Maybe I can learn just enough on the journey to understand that the door was worth going through, and I am honored that you are entering the water with me.

My journey with Trisha could not be as complete without the profound friendship with Archangel Raphael, who came into both of lives after my first wife Barbara's death and told us, "It is about time." He was saying that only from the wide view that he has and knowing that we have had many lives together that intertwined with his. His loving guidance has created an environment for us to communicate his messages through our business of T Michael Healing Arts. From the start of my opening to Spirit, he has gently stepped into our energy fields with the touch of a parent. For that, I am very grateful. His influence in what I write is subtle, but I know that he plays a part in how I think about the world. My journey is ongoing, and my hope for you as a reader is that in some small way, this book can touch your heart and bring a small piece of the Angelic realms energy with it.

Thank you for journeying with us.

Chapter 1

SPIRITUAL

Starbucks Spirituality

I know that normal people don't necessarily do this, but come on, when did I ever say I was "normal." Starbucks is a destination for me when I take long walks. It is the halfway point of my walk, and getting a coffee is a kind of a pat on the back for me. So, when I started thinking about Starbucks coffee cups, the different-sized cups remind me of people. Yes, coffee cups! Each person has a space to be filled with different ingredients, hot and cold, sweetness, bold and mild, or just right.

    Think about it. Take one cup; fill it with a liquid; add flavoring, sugar, and cream; and stir. Sounds like a perfect metaphor for us. During our lives, we come into this world at one size and grow larger while, all the time, having different ingredients added to us, whether they are forced on us or by our choice.

During my life, I have added love from family and bruises and bumps that sometimes made my cup leak, but never broke down. I kept adding to my cup through school, work, family, and marriage, and believe it or not, it never overflowed. How is that possible? Probably because while new things were being added over time, some things were being drained off as I grew in beliefs, knowledge, fears, love, and, yes, spirituality.

I don't think that at any time we are ever given more than we can handle. I recently had a conversation with Archangel Raphael through a channeling and he described that I had an eye patch over my third eye. I believe that eye patch is a way that I prevent my cup from overfilling. That same week I was allowed a peek around the eye patch just enough to allow insight into my cup. Even though I sometimes trip and my beliefs, knowledge, and even spirituality slosh around, I always get to participate in the game and see the things I need to see.

Taking our gifts for granted and forgetting that we are being gently guided is easy. Very few of us have a full cup of Spirit instantaneously like my loving partner. I think they just gave her a Big Gulp–sized cup. For most of us, we must be satisfied that we choose the ingredients that will put together a drink we can live with all the while trying not to spill it.

So, next time you go into a coffee store, look at the cups; then look around you and see the people. What ingredients are you filled with that you can share with those around you? Enjoy and drink from Source, knowing that you will never be too full.

My Father's Hands

Flashbacks can bring comfort as well as sadness, and sometimes they can bring both at the same time. I remember sitting in church, and my hand was laying on my father's open palm. Even then, I seemed to be thinking with a detachment of an age that I did not possess, that these hands fit together so well yet do not match in size. I wanted to grow into the man my father was, and to me that meant those little fingers had a long way to go before reaching what I thought was maturity. I just remember being comforted by the size of his hand but at the same time wondering if I could grow into his strength. Little did I realize that it is not the size of the hand that gives you character but the depth of the soul that transmits comfort to those around you. I wanted his love and radiance of being, but I did not know it at the time.

Now, looking back, I question if I grew into the hands of my father by looking at my own life and wondering if I have been able to pass down that specialness of character, strength, and purpose to those around me. Things like life, economic hardships, love, loss, and conditions that seemingly are uncontrollable play a huge part in making people feel that they have not succeeded in matching their father's hands.

But really, what is important? That I remember and cherish what my father's hands meant to me gives me hope that more is at play in my life than being successful and having things to prove my worth. Passing down love, ideas, character, attitudes, and, yes, the size of my hands means something that my family can carry forward. After all, what should be passed along but the grace of love that we all had when we came into this life and go back to when the time is right.

Look at your father's hands and see what you will, but remember we all are one, and the hands we come from are big indeed.

Walk Away

Archangel Raphael told me to walk away from the Crock-Pot and let him work with the ingredients. Of course,

Chapter 1 - SPIRITUAL

he was using a metaphor to tell me to release my burdens to him.

So, as I am sitting here watching a butterfly circle around a fountain, I am amazed at the peace that is given to me by an Angel. How many times do we just keep going because it is the only thing we know? You cannot stop and smell the roses because the dog is really eyeing them. Most of us have been raised to keep going: don't stop; roses can be smelled when you are in that rocking chair.

But I am here to tell you that sitting in the sun and listening to the power of the waterfall and the children laughing, as well as having an Angel encouraging me to walk away from the Crock-Pot, are things I would just like to say thank you for.

Life as we know it is over in a split second. I am thinking of the song with the line "slow down, you move to fast; you got to make the morning last." I believe Archangel Raphael talks to everyone at the same time if you are willing to listen. So just in case you are not hearing anything right now, here is a suggestion. Walk away from your Crock-Pot. Let him work with the ingredients so you can come back later and enjoy the results. Peace

Walk in My Shoes

Sometimes I think of things that are out of left field, but usually some form of spiritual meaning is behind them. Did you ever walk somewhere and notice that people walking past you will not look at you? I did a scientific poll and discovered that about one in ten looks at me. Could it be because I was wearing a New York sweatshirt or had a day-old beard? Or did they sense I really am a sixty-plus-year-old man just out for a walk? *I do not know.*

Yes, I do believe that age, upbringing, past and present social interactions, sex/gender, and personality all play a role in whether a person feels comfortable in making eye contact. But what has this world come to when we allow our ego to make us believe that it is not right to look someone in the eye and say hi? I of course could not just let it drop. I decided that it had to be me, that I was wearing my invisible shield, and that people just did not see me. I also decided that it was all because I was holding my aura too close to my body. Testing this was very easy. I kept walking but focused on expanding my auric field, intentionally reaching it out to slap others' fields as I approached. Guess what—it worked. As soon as I took this approach, people started seeing me and saying hi.

Knowing that you do have control over your energy field and can have a positive impact on someone else who isn't even aware of it is quite fascinating. No need for ego or control; just an honest exchange or energy. Just your knowing is enough. Try it out and let me know how it goes. It seems that a thought from left field regarding Spiritual matters hits a home run again. By the way, I did a second poll: nine out of ten people looked at me and said something. Go figure. The results are within an error rate of 50 percent and are not subject to any scientific certainty, and no auric fields were harmed in the transmission of energy.

Flash of Time

Born into this world
through a flash of
brilliant light,
opened a world
of trial and error.

The trials come from the many
opportunities to learn as I grew.
Not good or bad, but moments of reflection
to determine the path taken in developing the soul
that chose to be here.

The errors just helped to self-correct
the trajectory to keep me on the path of
self-discovery.

Growing older is just another reminder that
I have a time frame to complete the mission
set up when I flashed into existence.

The excitement of self-discovery is that it opens
avenues to be more at peace and lead me
to meet the special people in my life like you.

Chapter 1 - SPIRITUAL

On this day of celebrating my entry into the light,
I wish all humans on this planet a joyous birthday that created
their own entry into this soup we call form.
I celebrate with the mass consciousness
that we all participate in and extend my energy
to you in thanks.

You Don't Know What It Feels Like to Be in Someone Else's Shoes Unless You Wear Them

We take our understanding of having the ability to put ourselves in someone else's shoes for granted. We think we can do it, but it takes a very empathetic person who cannot only mentally feel the other person but also understand the subtleties and nuances of that person's life at the cellular level. We all say that we care, that we love, that we understand another's life because secretly we want to make that person into us. But when it comes down to it, most of us, even those with spiritual insight, do not really feel for another as if we were in their shoes.

The reason is that our ego is too strong, and we take the road that our will be done is the one that should be traveled because it is the only one we know. There is no right or wrong in this equation. This is something I've noticed in myself as well as many other people. After all, we come into this world to carry out our own alpha and omega or beginning and ending. Doing that is hard enough without stepping into someone else's shoes and trying to work their story as well.

But I believe with all my heart that we have the capability to at least understand what people are feeling. It is not our job to fix others, so to speak. But to understand and wear their shoes for only a moment will reveal that when you let go of all your own prejudices, expectations, and conditioning, you just might feel something that is not your own. You might only identify as belonging to another's feelings, and for the first time in a long time, you can react from the heart and know that you really understand where this person is coming from. Does it mean that you must take it on? No, of course not. But I believe it means that you have connected to Spirit in the most elemental way. At the cellular level, you have been touched and care about something or someone who does not meet your way of explaining life.

When trying to walk in someone else's shoes, so to speak, consider the following:

1. Care to listen without trying to control the conversation.
2. Feel beyond your own conditioning.
3. Open the door to new possibilities that, maybe, your way is not the only way.
4. Let your heart move you to the right course of action.
5. Use your intuitive senses to see, hear, know, and feel an understanding that takes you out of your own comfort zone.
6. Wear someone else's shoes for the first time with grace and patience to become aware that we do not have all the answers and be okay with that.

7. Allow that crack in your armor to open and be the lesson that you need at this moment.
8. Dance in the shadows of another and bring in the light that is needed.
9. Sing to someone else's soul in the key that only they can hear without worry about how you will be viewed.
10. Love without conditions until you know that they see it.

Only when we let go, completely fall into Spirit, and share that with everyone around us will we truly understand the meaning of walking in someone else's shoes.

What Is in a Birthday?

The same plants grow, and the same water flows down the channel made by human hands of the past. You wake up with the same light shining on your face, trying to beat the alarm from shaking you out of bed. You bring coffee to your love and follow the same routine created through countless lives throughout the time of humanity on this planet.

Why is one birthday any different than any other one that has manipulated you into thinking that you are getting older when, in fact, we know we make time up in the first place?

I was thinking about this one time as my birthday slowly crept toward me, and even though I was trying to ignore it, with the help of those around me, I couldn't ignore the fact that the day had arrived that told the world that I was now sixty-three. So I decided to confront this confusion head-on and try to determine what it meant for me to face myself in a mirror and figure this out once and for all.

In a time when I see friends my age retiring, I find myself in the middle of a third career. I would never have imagined that being an author at this age was even a reality, let alone a choice. Grandma Moses is my role model.

And then there are the adventures with Spirit. Who would have thought that Spirit could come into a person's life, open the door, and say, "It is your turn to travel this road with us and to learn to be in tune like so many that have come before you." Personally, I think my friends could have looked in the same mirror I am and decided that it was not worth the effort. But not me; thanks to the forces that we can't sense with our physical body, the powers of the unseen decided this middle-class banker should go on an adventurous mission with them and report the messages of the ages that they have been trying to communicate to humanity since the explosion of life.

I am truly honored that I can do this and know I have a purpose and that Spirit, Angels and Guides believe in me and think that I can do my part in communicating these messages. Ultimately, love and forgiveness are the underlying meanings behind all the messages, which help us all get back to where we started.

So, as I sit here on my so-called birthday, I thank them for the opportunity and wish you all happy birthday on your day and hope that you can connect in your own ways to something that feels like your own mission. Age, I have discovered, means nothing when you are following your joy. Enjoy the ride and watch out for mirrors.

Chapter 1 - SPIRITUAL

To Remember

*Sentimentally speaking,
looking at the past does not shed light
on the future.*

*What it does do is give a peace within
the framework of safety.*

*Knowing that the journey begins now,
no matter what transpired in the past,
brings comfort to the Spirit and helps
to shed the ego-controlled world.*

*Move forward in peace,
knowing that the hug from Heaven
guides you on your journey to take
you back to the start of remembrance.*

Look Closer

The next time you are around a tree; and if you cannot remember what a tree is, those are things that stand around and have green things hanging from their arms. They sometimes slap you in the face as you walk by and are not paying attention to them. They like to soak up water and reward you if you feed them well. If you do not feed and water them, they let you know by disappearing into themselves, dropping their crap all over the place, and by laughing at you while you clean up after them. All they have ever wanted was for you to pay attention to them, and if you do, they will heap all kinds of love your way. I must have taught this to my kids when they were young because you can always find one of them hugging a tree while on a hike. Conditioning works.

Look closer at a tree and you find the veins of life flowing through their greenness. All the leaves act in unison around one simple idea: to live—to spread their roots, to bud and to multiply. It really doesn't get any simpler than that.

Trees dry out, blow in the wind, react to unwanted chemicals and are made up of the same building blocks as everything else. They flower with sometimes beautiful creations that attract love, sharing, and pollination. Then in the fall, they drop whatever is holding onto them and wait for the extremes of weather to take over before exploding with life all over again in the spring.

Sound familiar? Humans are not unlike trees. You can get slapped if you are not paying attention. If we are well fed and watered, we flourish, but if not, we shrivel. If we are not paid attention to, we tend to crap all over and watch the consequences. Look closer at a human and you will see the life flowing through them. We only want to live, spread our message, and multiply. If we are fed, watered, nourished, and loved, we bloom into a unique form that likes to share with others for the most part. But watch out if we are not nourished because then we can see the alternative or ugly side of being a human.

Humans like trees are meant to sway in the breeze and not break. We are meant to put on a grand show and attract attention. Being an individual is our right but being part of the whole is our mission. How we get there is extremely difficult at times, and honestly, we do not do this well at times. We don't seem to learn from experience and the cycles of our lives appear to be more of a trial than a passion.

Humans can learn a lot from the tree by focusing on the following:
1. Reach out gently.
2. Share the nourishment with those around you.

3. Handle the changes in the environment with dignity and focus.
4. Be one with the community and coexist as if life matters.
5. Communicate on the breeze without expecting anything in return.
6. Know that all life matters and play nice.
7. Share the air in a way that benefits all.
8. Understand that you have been put here for a reason and know where you fit in.
9. It is okay to expose yourself and show that you are vulnerable.
10. Through your actions, you will give and take, but giving your beauty enhances everyone and everything.

The next time you are around a tree, look closer, give it a hug, say thank you for the great life lessons, and listen or feel in your heart for a response from the universe.

How Great Thou Art

For the last day, this one line—how great thou art—has been going through my head until I finally paid attention to it. Now, I mentioned that I grew up in the church but was never what I would call overly religious. Even at a young age,

Chapter 1 - SPIRITUAL

I thought there had to be more. So, as I got older and fell into Spirituality, it fit my Soul like peanut butter goes with jam for a sandwich.

I admit that the music to this line kept humming in my mind, and with an increasing annoyance and a lack of understanding why this was happening to someone who knew religion didn't hold all the answers, I realized that I needed to pay attention to this and try to figure it out, if only to get it out of my head.

I thought of the song and quickly concluded that the words to the song did not point me in the right direction. So, I focused on just those four words and tried to figure out how I felt about them. At first, I kept returning to my thought that it had to be about God, but it did not settle right in my heart. Not that thinking about God isn't okay, but why did these four words want me to go in another direction? I am sure you are ahead of me, but when I am focused on a problem, I sometimes only see a tree instead of the forest.

In my case, it hit me literally between the eyes, and Spirit said, "Wake up. How great thou art." Me? What? This is what Spirit was trying to say? Of course, my ego wanted it to all be about me. Coming off that pedestal, I realized what was being said: that me, you, and everyone are great from the Spiritual viewpoint; that we sometimes get caught into the narrow views of what is going on around us and forget to realize that we are great as individuals; and that we are great as directors of our own destinies here. There is no one else, just us.

Wow, it took me a while to get there, but that revelation did feel good in my heart, and I will try to remember that lesson as I move forward. Spirit also wants you to remember that it is okay to focus on yourself and to reflect on the reality of how great you are instead of always worrying about others. Be selfish for once.

Now the song means so much more to me, and I guess that it does not have to play over and over in my mind—although I like it.

Beneath the Surface

Watching a giant tanker move down the Columbia River under the Astoria Bridge made me realize that I know nothing about this river. Looking at it from high up on the hills, I saw dark patches in the water, which I think reflects the water's depth. It turns out the explanation my son, the oceanographer, gave me made more sense. He explained that the patches are algae colonies that turn the river red. Sure, enough, as I looked closer, I saw red patches everywhere and the beauty of the river with these color swatches in the water.

Chapter 1 - SPIRITUAL

It made me think that we never know what is below the surface.

Take ourselves, for instance. What we show on the surface is usually one thing, and we are not necessarily good at showing those around us what is really going on below. We could have emotional issues that run as deep as the gravel riverbed only to be brought to the surface by some giant ship traveling by and churning everything up.

I think Spirit is like the algae colonies. It floats on the surface, stretches out its energy in all directions, radiates its color in the sun, and infuses power and sustenance to all around that need the help. You can enjoy the beauty of its miracle and grow with it, or you can totally ignore its presence. Allowing ourselves to be open to Spirit in any way can maybe move the waves and churn up what is below the surface in hopefully a gentle way that will allow the color, power, energy, and love enter our lives.

I think I am going to pay more attention to what is below my surface and make sure that I am not missing an opportunity to float with the algae. What is below the surface for you? Do you allow Spirit to float in your space and gently ride its waves as you move through space?

Stand Tall

Reach towards the sky,
and bring sunlight to your structure.

Find passion in what you do,
and believe in who you are.

Send out love in all directions
without the expectation
that it will be sent back.

Remember the reason that you are here
and do your best
to live up to the plan.

Be the tree of your world
despite what may be going on around you,
your brilliance will have an effect
on those that come into your energy field.

So, stand tall and reach high
to be all that you dreamed of
before you arrived.

Chapter 1 - SPIRITUAL

Our Amnesia to Spirit

During a recent surgery, I was placed under general anesthesia. No big deal; it is done thousands of times a day across the world. What I kept pondering afterward was the amnesia produced. I can very clearly remember being pushed toward the operating room and reading the signs along the way. The person pushing me to the operating room even asked if I thought I was capable of moving myself from one table to another once we got to the room. Sure, no problem. I thought I was fine, not helpless. As we entered the room, I saw the table and a couple of people working on the other side of the room. Then the amnesia took over; I do not remember anything until about nine hours later when my wife and my son came walking through the curtains into my room.

A few gifted among us can see beyond the curtain and what is going on. Trisha told me that there was a two-hour period during the surgery when I left my body and had a big reunion with family and Guides. I had also talked to Archangel Raphael before my surgery and voiced my concern that I did not want to disconnect from Spirit while I was under. He very gently reassured me that my Spirit is whole and can never disconnect. He said that I would leave my body and attend this meeting and suggested I try to remember it.

So, in a weird way, I was kind of ready to go to see what would happen and what I could remember. How fascinating, but no—I do not remember squat between the operating door being open and seeing my family. Dang.

This event reminds me of our relationship with Spirit. Most of us have amnesia because we cannot remember the moment before we came into this world or what we are going back to. Do not get me wrong. I think it is all part of the plan. I do not think of it as a missed opportunity but more as a chance to remember at some point during meditation or sleep. My point is that the veil is so much thinner than we think. I believe this is how close we are to remembering the moment before we came into this world with plans, hopes, and dreams of what we would like to accomplish this time around—so close yet still waiting for the veil to lift to see what is on the other side. I, for one, plan to continue to seek and clear the cloud of my amnesia.

I think that you can relate to the amnesia to Spirit through your own life stories. Just by understanding that the veil is so thin, and creating your own way to lift that veil, you will connect in a way to Spirit that will change your life. This can be accomplished by you in various ways such as meditation, yoga, learning about intuition and the Clair-senses, or just asking the Angels or your Guides as you fall asleep at night to show you the way to Spirit.

Chapter 1 - SPIRITUAL

A Rainbow in the Storm

As I usually do, I woke early and went about my morning flow of habit as if on a puppet string. Not awake or asleep and being somewhere in between, I had a sense that something was different about this morning. I realized that the color of everything inside and out had taken on an orange hue that made me take notice. The first thought that came to mind was a tornado. I don't know why, but Dorothy from *The Wizard of Oz* popped into my head, making me laugh.

My desk faces an outside window that I can look out and admire the trees and birds, but everything outside was so eerily quiet it woke me up even more. I decided that something was going on and it was time to investigate. What I have learned over the last five years of studying intuition and not necessarily thinking that I am good at it is to pay attention to what is going on around me. Taking my own advice of not becoming so entrenched in my physical surroundings that I don't notice the miracles happening around me all the time, I walked to the front door, opened it, and was surprised to see it was raining. That shouldn't be much of a surprise in Oregon, but I had just looked at the weather report and didn't see rain in the forecast.

Opening the front door really was like what Dorothy saw when she opened the door of her house after landing and the movie went from black-and-white to color because what was directly in front of me in full Technicolor was a massive double rainbow. I do not have to tell you that I was very thankful that I was listening to my intuition that morning. Standing in the rain and taking pictures of this magnificent phenomenon while cars drove by, their owners seemingly not noticing it, opened all my senses. The colors grew brighter and bolder while at the same time my heart responded in kind. Sitting on the porch and taking it all in, I thanked my guides, angels, parents, family, deceased dog, and, of course, Absolute Love.

Tears of joy at the sight of the rainbow, when authentic, are so healing because they make you feel that there is more to life than the mundane daily rituals while at the same time reminding you to pay attention and take stock of who you are and that you are here for a passion that only you can feel. At least that is what I felt at the time, and I am sure that when those types of things happen to you, it will register with you differently.

I knew that this event was directed by Spirit especially for me, and I took it that way. I took it as a sign that all is well and that great things have and will happen. The Angels know that I am a visual person who really likes to not only see evidence but feel it as well. For me, it makes my doubting Thomas rest in peace. Now I know that you can say that this rainbow was just coincidence, and scientifically speaking, you would be right. But free will and choice allow me to choose my results and meaning, so I chose to think Divine intervention is the cause and to respond as if I have seen the face of God. I know it might be overkill, but why is it ever wrong to read things into what you would consider profound Spiritual events and allow yourself to be energized with energy, love, and the healing grace of Spirit?

You might want to try it yourself the next time something so beautiful enters your life, slaps you across the face, wakes you up, and dares you to pay attention. If nothing else, Dorothy and the Wizard would be proud of you taking the time to notice.

The Miracle of Now

> **Miracle**—an effect in the physical world which surpasses all known human or natural powers and is therefore ascribed to supernatural agency.

I have been putting a lot of thought into what I think a miracle is and whether what happened to me recently could be classified as a miracle. The event itself is not important. It made me consider what the definition of a miracle is and why we don't see more miracles.

I have a theory. A thought occurred to me that if we are always looking to the future for a miracle, we will miss the one right in front of us. As humans, we are always asking for things to happen in the future and are sometimes disappointed when they do not happen. It seems obvious to me that if we ask for a future miracle, we will probably get it in the future, just not in our concept of time. It also occurred to me that I should be focused on now, not the future. In my way of thinking, the moment of now is more important because it is staring me in the face, and I can react to it now. I mean, really, if you think about it, we cannot predict even five minutes from now, so why not pay attention to the miracles happening all around us now? By intuitively using the skills we have all been given through our feelings and thoughts, the miracle is not that they don't exist; it is that we choose to not see what is going on around us.

A great definition came from my partner, Trisha. She said that a miracle is "a change in perspective." That blew me away. My whole life I had been looking for those things that could not be explained and labeling them miracles. Instead, I could have just changed my perspective and looked at things differently and realized there are a lot more miracles in my now than I thought there ever were.

According to Neal Donald Walsh in *Conversations with God*, feelings are the language of the Soul, followed by thoughts and finally words. I believe this is all about intuition, and by using our feelings, thoughts, and words through seeing, feeling, knowing, and hearing at the Soul level, we can open ourselves to the miracle that we all are. Just think about it. Your intuition skills cannot necessarily be explained scientifically, at least to the satisfaction of that community, but according to the definition of a miracle, intuition does have an impact on the physical world but surpasses our known understanding.

We are all bundles of miracles just waiting to pronounce to the world that we understand our Soul's connection and that we will see what is here, right now, in front of us. So, the next time someone asks if you have seen a miracle, say yes and mean it, knowing that you fit the definition and that all of us can use our intuition skills to go beyond the veil of the scientific rational mind.

Enjoy the journey.

The Spiritual Dandelion

I admit that I have a few dandelions in my yard even though my next-door neighbor has made it his life's mission to eradicate this lowly little flower. *Dandelion* in the dictionary means "lion's mane," and although I never put much thought to where it got its name, it seems very appropriate. If you take the time to look at it, it does look like it could belong to a lion.

To me, dandelions are like Spirit. They do not need to be pollinated and can grow pretty much wherever they land. You can try to eradicate them, but isn't it funny how they always come back? They can be pretty if you take the time to get to know them, and boy, they will multiply if given the chance. Certainly, we all have played with them when they morphed into white clouds of little parachutes floating in the wind.

How perfect. You do not have to feed and water them and they multiply whether you are paying attention to them or not. They challenge you to ignore them, and as a bonus, they spread their knowledge to all points of the compass in the hopes of just getting someone to notice and realize that they truly are amazing.

We can learn some things about Spirit from the dandelion:

1. They come in a bright color with a broad, leafy base, saying, "Look at me."
2. No matter what we try to do to them, they just gently keep coming back.
3. Given the opportunity, they will multiply until there is no way that you can ignore them.

4. You can partake in their energy by absorbing a part or all of them.
5. They do not take no for an answer. When they want you to notice them, they get your attention.
6. Being around a dandelion makes me happy. They are so simple yet so complicated.
7. You can poison them by thinking that you do not need them in your life, but guess what? They are patient and will return.
8. If you block out your world by filling it in with concrete, the dandelion will grow in the cracks.

So, lessons learned. Even the lowly dandelion is a miracle if you give it half a chance. Open your heart and let the miracles around you be noticed. Like a dandelion, allow Spirit to land where it wants. Enjoy the amazing opportunities that Spirit brings to you and do not forget at the end of the day to thank Spirit for its contribution to your journey.

Coming to the Center

*Attraction without feeling does not work
in the Law of the Universe.
Only when you come to the center of your feelings,
and balance with
what feels right in the alignment of thought,
can the hope of
achievement be felt.*

*Walking hand in hand with yourself and
directing your thoughts with
feelings before you make decisions and speak,
will empower the energy to
give you what you want.*

*The Law of Attraction is there for everyone,
waiting in the wings of the
angels to pronounce that understanding comes
with true knowledge.
Being one with your feelings and aligning with Spirit
will show the
hidden steppingstones that were there the whole time.*

*So, breathe in the peace of Spirit and know
that your feelings will truly
align you to bring in what you seek and melt away
the ego's grasp of
your lack mentality.*

*In this dream you have more control over the outcome
than what you think.
Go into the future knowing that Spirit
will always point you in
the right direction and that the outcome is assured.*

The Wear Marks of Life

Walk through any forest along a well-worn trail, and you are likely to see are wear marks on the trail side of the trees. I never thought about this until my oldest son and I were hiking through a forest in the Northwest and he pointed out this phenomenon. Now I have been walking through forests for years, and I have had many hugging encounters with trees as well as gentle touching worn bark. It was as if I was being called to connect in some fashion that I thought only meant something to me. But I realize that stepping back and being shown the wear marks prove that other people in the world touch and hug trees as well. Why did I not see it before?

I believe I know the answer to that. Until you open up Spiritually and really sense the energy around you, staying in a protected cocoon of individuality controlled by the ego and the belief that you are the only one that could be possibly be affected by the beauty of a tree is easy. Having been on the Spiritual path for so many years, I see more, feel more, hear more, and know more. That is why that day with my son in the forest, the trees and shrubs were brilliant in light and color, so much so that they were almost blinding. When we came to a small grove of redwoods, I was almost overwhelmed by the profound beauty of their design and the smell of the Earth. It was as if I were part of the Earth, and even though it was an overcast day, the energy coming from this area was very noticeable.

To me, Spirit intentionally sends signals like, color, smells, and sounds our way to get out attention. We all have wear marks from Spirit coming close to us by their touching, hugging, and trying to communicate in a gentle but brilliant way. Think about your years here and the many times you have probably said that something is so beautiful, is colorful, smells incredible, tastes wonderful but never tied it to Spirit.

Allow yourself to be a tree along the trail. As Spirit comes by to touch you, take it in proudly and openly thank it for the attention in helping you grow into the amazing tree that you are. Grow tall in knowing that with help, you can spread your branches and become a beacon to the community around you. Wear marks are only noticeable on you if you open your heart and sense the gentle way that Spirit interacts with you every day.

Enjoy the blinding nature of Spirit reaching out to you, and you will be surprised how often it happens.

The Still, Small Voice

At one time or the other, all of us have had a profoundly moving experience. The way the sunlight shines through the trees and creates a rainbow star in your vision as you move your head. The way the breeze moves through and caresses the wind chimes into a symphony that you swear you have heard before but not in this lifetime. The way the hummingbird slowly glides up to you, looks you in the eyes, seems to understand what you are feeling, and then darts off in a blinding flash. The way the sound of water flowing from its source in the garden mixing with the rustling sounds of grass, bushes, and trees drifts through my brain cells, making you feel loved by the earth. Put it all together and you have an intuitive orchestra that connects to that still, small voice that says we are not alone.

How often do these events happen? I am guessing that they could happen often, but we are moving too fast in this linear world to notice. I, for one, sometimes find myself doing this job and that job, going here and there, and not finding the time to hearing the symphony. Wouldn't it be nice to set aside one period a day dedicated to listening for the music?

Profoundly moving experiences come in all shapes and sizes. You do not have to be special to have one. You just need to be open to the possibilities that Spirit is here and all around, hoping you will slow down and notice. Put a smile on your face, don't worry about the tear in your eye, and go out and have your own moving experience. Remember, though, to say thank you to the ones providing the symphony. They are listening, and however, my thought is that they do not want your thanks, just you to notice what has been placed before you.

In the Eyes of Spirit

When in moments of uncertainty you find yourself sitting and reflecting about could have, would have, or should have, and you reflect on your life as if you are looking from above at someone else, that is a powerful moment to ask yourself why it matters. Spirit has a way of giving you exactly what you need at exactly the right time whether it meets your human need to control the outcome or not.

Recently I went through a hypnosis session. that I had preconceived notions about what I would like to get out of it. During this session, my goal was to find out what happened during a recent surgery in the time that amnesia took over because of the drugs introduced. I was sure that it mattered for me to know where I went during two hours that my Soul apparently decided it needed to leave my body and go to a place to talk with what I call my "board," which is made up of deceased relatives, Guides, Angels, and others who help direct my life.

Spirit had other ideas. I found myself in a beautiful meadow, knowing that I was surrounded by the board despite not seeing them. Frustration was setting in because, again, as a human, I wanted to control things, and the experience was not happening the way I wanted it to. Looking up to the right in the sky, I saw what looked like a star coming toward me. It stopped and hovered in front of me and honestly reminded me of a scene in John Travolta's movie *Phenomenon*. I guess that the being felt that I needed a very visual experience. No words were spoken, but I knew that this was one of my Guardian Angels, Theron. He leaned forward in all his energy-ball perfection and touched my third eye with his forehead. The explosive power of his pure energy entered through my opened third eye, traveled down through my body, and turned me into what I can only describe as a Light Being. My human form was there but resembled a long-haired warrior with chest armor. The image reminded me of the sixties when most of us had long hair and carried the persona of invincibility.

The gist of the conversation was that the missing time was not as important as I thought. This moment with Theron, seeing that humans are Light Beings and profoundly beautiful, was what The Board wanted me to know. How I got here was unimportant. Yes, the surgery needed to happen to fix the physical body, but the vision of who I truly am at the Soul level is what Theron wanted me to see. He told and showed me that this message of what we all are at our core level and

Chapter 1 - SPIRITUAL

where we came from is my mission statement, so to speak. He said that it was time humans woke up and saw themselves as they really are. We are not just the physical body as we go about being human on Earth. We are much more than that. Ultimately, we all go home as Light Beings and join the oneness.

He told me other things, but being a Light Being seemed to be the message that I am supposed to pass along at this point. His hug and release to return made me sad in one respect, but it also made me realize that humans try to control far too many things. I do not really need to know what happened during the missing time because reflecting on the what-ifs or the would-of, could-of moments in anyone's life is so unimportant. Seeing yourself for who you truly are makes you stop, take a breath, and reflect on what is important. This will be different for each of us, but one thing is the same: we are all more than we thought.

I, as a human, would still like to know about that missing time, but I can now be satisfied in knowing that if I need to know, that information will be shared with me in due course. By seeing the past, present, and future all in one vision, I can relax into the arms of Spirit.

Even if you never go through hypnosis and meet yourself through your Guardian Angel, what is important to know is that you are much more than you think, and that, my friends, should give you strength that no matter what happens in this life for you through your physicality of being in form, you can count on one thing. We look good in armor and long hair. Plus, what a trip to look forward to. Far out—no really, far out.

Wanting a Spiritual Experience

One of the most profound experiences in my life was snorkeling with turtles and a squad of squid. It transcended my understanding of what having a Spiritual experience would be like. Why is that? My expectation of having a Spiritual experience like those over the centuries where people fall to the ground and see blinding lights would not have to be so dramatic. I could think of many things that would make me feel like I had been selected to see, hear, and feel a moment so exciting that it would be like permanent goosebumps. I am not that complicated, so I do not require anything but a simple and less complicated viewing that I would know was out of the realm of normal and would have no choice of accepting the event as a Spiritual experience.

For example, the following would be definitive for me:
1. When I'm disc golfing, throwing a disc and having it go straight to the hole and—to take it further—drop into the cage in one throw without seeing it fly back

over my head in the wrong direction as I casually explain that the wind caught it at a twenty-six-degree angle and lifted it right into that unsuspecting seagull.
2. Climbing to the second floor of my house to clean out the gutters so easily that I can walk right along the edge without falling off instead of holding on for dear life as my white knuckles go numb and I inch toward the edge of the roof while saying some sort of mantra to anyone that will listen.
3. Cutting down a tree and having it fall exactly where I calculated it would fall and break apart into small pieces that I could easily stack instead of seeing the tree go the wrong way and if I would have only built that shed in a different spot.
4. Crabbing where nothing goes wrong and catching the limit as opposed to seeing the crab pot arching over my head while I stand in the water with my camera thinking that I should grab the end of the crab pot line that a friend is obviously not holding onto.

These are just some things that I would think would make me personally feel like I was having a Spiritual experience, which is all I have ever wanted. Somewhere deep down, I can remember thinking as a kid that I would like to experience something like the apparitions seen at Our Lady of Fatima. I mean, come on, wouldn't it be so cool to have that kind of experience? Being the reporter type, I could think of nothing more fun than interviewing Spirit, Angels and Guides that are visiting and writing about the experience. But I digress. I want to believe that such experiences are available for all of us instead of a select few. Not that I am jealous, but I look forward to my own experience of blinding light, incredible beauty, and joyous connection. Is this expecting too much? I don't think so. I believe, as I have been told, all people are connected and can have these types of experiences if they only believe. I am telling you right now that I believe I can and so can you.

    Just believe. Reach out and touch Spirit in a way that there is no way that the Angels and Guides can misunderstand your readiness to participate. And maybe, just maybe, something will happen to remind you of your own definition of what a Spiritual experience is. I hope to get there soon myself so I can write about something that has a definition instead of wishful thinking. I will let you know if it happens for me, but in the meantime, let us all reach out and make the attempt. After all, we have been told many times that all we must do is ask. May you have the Spiritual experience of a lifetime, and if you ever see turtles or squid swimming in the ocean, you made it.

The Birth

*Swirling within the crystal reflections
to meet the Spirit of forever,
brings the journey of separation.*

*Many lives, many experiences,
create a bond
that was meant to be,
but broken into many stories.*

*Persia's colors and textures,
weaving into a tapestry of love
and faith,
being one of many but
always the first bond.*

*Tibet's special closeness
through the friendship of sacrifice,
created a continued spiritual
connection brought down through the ages.*

*American Indian relationship
held fast with the strength
of Spirit and love
provided comfort
within the pride of land
and animal.*

*The English mansion
with the stairway to
remembering the closeness
of the past lives together.*

*Only in the original birth
did the creation of the
destinies come together
to form an unbroken
bond of swirling energy
that lasted through lifetimes
and followed us home.*

Chapter 1 - SPIRITUAL

The Soul's Journey

What are we but souls who enter this space to achieve an unknown source of continued movement toward the freedom to not enter this space. On the wheel of life, humans go around and around in the hope that they will get somewhere, but if we just stop and think about it, we are already there. We really don't have to do anything to be accepted back into Source because we never really left. It creates quite a conundrum for all us humans, running around in our daily lives trying to accomplish something. Most don't really think about it, but for those who do, we sometimes wonder why we work so hard to get to a place of guaranteed entrance.

I was thinking about becoming a grandfather for the first time, and it occurred to me that this Soul that is coming in has chosen its parents for a reason. We don't ever really know what the reason is because it was a contract established long ago by that Soul for purposes only it knows. But that one Soul coming in now affects so many around it who feel they know what is best for it and will raise the little one with love while trying to guide him or her to become one of the humans on the wheel. Little do any of us suspect that this Soul's course has already been laid out and that, although we as parents do our best, really what it comes down to is that Soul had a plan all along that, more than likely, will get carried out in the allotted time.

Wow, being caretakers of sorts creates a picture in the mind that we are truly only there to guide and sometimes protect these little people knowing that in the end it will all be perfect and that that Soul will achieve what it wants to if not in this lifetime, then another.

Putting this all into perspective, my becoming a grandfather means so much more. It means really getting to know this person from a Spiritual level as well as a human level, loving this person from a perspective that connects lifetimes upon lifetimes, instead of the short time in this incarnation. This is big-picture stuff, and taken from that vantage point, it could be overwhelming. But then again, holding this grandchild's hand and walking through the forest while talking about birds could be all that is required. Just knowing that this grandchild's Soul allows me into their spiritual adventure is good enough for me, as well as finding the strength to pass along wisdom that was passed down to me by my father will allow me to at least think that I can play a role in their lives that means something.

The important thing is to know that even though this little one in this incarnation has come with the full knowledge of Source, love on both sides is all that is needed to keep the flow of what is important alive, and that looking at the big picture is not always needed when you look into the eyes of a child.

My Way Is the Best Way

Following the fine, graceful lines of the chair, I have spent hours delicately sanding it in a restoration attempt. I had made it years ago out of cedar, and it was an act of love. The feel of the wood, the grain patterns, and the smell, without question, sent me back to woodshop where I was taught the balance of not taking enough time or taking too much time. So, seeing my chair's surface looking saddened by weather and age, I decided that only I, super-woodsman, could restore her to the remarkable sitting instrument she deserves to be.

Hours later, I wondered why, covered in dust, I look like Santa and had sore muscles from hand sanding. I sensed someone watching me, and slowly I turned and saw—yes, you guessed it—my phone. It was calling me to ask Google if there was a better way.

Did you know that there are wood strippers that, when applied right, work in about ten minutes? I know what you are thinking. Some of you are saying, "No ... how could you?" Then, there are those saying that I am a little slow in the head and should have thought of that a long time ago.

Isn't this also true about Spiritual matters? Some people seem to know and feel everything and have taken years to acquire Spiritual knowledge. Then others seem to be handed their knowledge without really trying or understanding it. They just do and assume we can all do it too.

Spirit is like the chair. There are many ways to get to the same conclusion, meaning, source, lesson, or finished chair. No one way is better. They all get you to the end.

So, my chair will be beautiful and will reflect me in its graceful lines, and as I sit on its soft wood, you can guess what I am going to say: I did it my way.

Controlling Faith

That title feels like an oxymoron to me. How can you control faith? *Faith*, according to Wikipedia, is "confidence or trust in a person, thing, deity, view, or in the doctrines or teachings of a religion. It can be defined as belief that is not based on proof." I like to tell myself that I have the faith to move mountains. The belief I have in Angels and my friend Archangel Raphael is based mostly on faith, although I have to say that, at times, things happen that appear to me to be physical in nature. Deep down, I have always been a "show me" person. I want to see and touch something before I completely believe. I would have been a good resident in the

Chapter 1 - SPIRITUAL

"Show-Me" State. My personality normally requires me to be in control about decisions and forward momentum so that I can feel part of the equation, not just a reactionary force to whatever is going on. But as I have gotten older and now fall into that senior category, I am realizing that I have very little control over things that matter to me, like spirituality. So, this is a conflict within my psyche where my need for control has to give over to my desire for faith. After all, when you are closer to the end zone of life, you start thinking about these questions, and at least for me, faith has become a bigger issue.

Archangel Raphael was trying to explain to me that faith was letting go of all the stuff that seems to be crumbling around me, and he said to place trust in him to help make decisions first so that I could follow the dots of awareness and accomplish my divine blueprint. He gave me the example of a Crock-Pot. You combine different ingredients and set a timer, and you walk away and come back later. What you get is a beautiful dinner. His implication was that I needed to let go of my control issues about things going on around me and let them go to him. Walk away and come back later.

Faith in him allows me to release my control and job it out for him to work on the solution. I, of course, have free will to choose solutions that I want, but if we can indeed job out things to the Angels and let them work on solutions while we work on falling into faith, then doesn't this sound a whole lot more relaxing? Is it really that simple? Are we as humans with our life purposes that we came to accomplish making things so much more complicated than they need to be? I guess I am willing to find out. I believe that I can still control my destiny but within the boundaries of turning on my faith button and really believing at the core of my being that I am getting help from Spirit. After all, is there a way to prove that faith does not work?

If I were to pass along any advice, it would be to give faith a shot: stir the ingredients of the Crock-Pot once in a while but walk away and come back later.

Seeing Stars

There are moments in everyone's life that we just absolutely, positively, without a doubt know that it means something. Not only do we pay attention to the moment, but we also put our feelings into it, which creates an even stronger bond between us and the event. I believe that most of us are so busy with the day-to-day human existence that we don't really reflect on these events. We forget what it was we wanted to remember when we decided to come here again. But exactly these moments of intense and sudden impact should shock us into the wonderment of living up to the contract we created for ourselves. Granted, when you are a child, these events didn't always snap you into thinking at the level of the soul, but reflective thinking combined with a series of life events and a more mature thinking process put a different spin on life.

I learned very early in life that "seeing stars" did not always mean looking up at a night sky. "Seeing stars" sometimes could just simply mean that your brother took a swing with a golf club and your head just happened to be in the way of his backswing. Even when I was a three-year-old, that I could see things swirling around my head that were hard to explain became suddenly very clear. Flooding the bathroom because I could reach the sink and seeing the reflective shock in my grandmother's eyes make a kid think. Watching the so-called witch of Omaha work in her run-down yard I realized that she was just an elderly person trying to get by and thought for the first time about age. Realizing that in Panama someone created snakes and placed them in front of me in the dark to scare the bejesus out of me made me think that I, along with Indiana Jones, don't really like snakes and that walking down the center of the street makes the odds more in my favor, especially if you can run fast when a car comes along and lights up the road. Riding on the handlebars of a bicycle that your brother is driving downhill and decides to brake is one of those events that make you sees stars especially after he runs over your midsection. I decided right then and there that walking was a great thing.

Other than my brother trying to kill me along the way, I believe that all these events and others like them have been important in keeping me interested and on track, so to speak. I believe that by having moments that light up my world and made me think something profound at the time allowed me to continue along the path, moving toward whatever it is I decided was my life purpose. Paying attention along the way becomes the challenge because it is so easy to blow off what time tells us is unimportant. But without these life events to help mold and guide us, we may need to keep coming back. I don't know about you, but if it helps to reflect on these events to prevent a repeat performance, I am all for it.

So, seeing stars is not so bad if, as my mother said many times, it knocks some sense into you. Thanks, Mom. I like the lessons but could do with a little less of the pain.

Open your heart to the life lessons given to you and see if you can weave a story line that helps you connect to your purpose. Good luck, and duck if you see the club coming at you.

Chapter 1 - SPIRITUAL

When Does Life Really Begin?

Think through the stages of your life and reflect on the moments when you had a spark of some kind that changed your trajectory. For instance, when I was little in England while my father was stationed there as part of the Air Force, a spark comes to mind as my father was helping me off the ground and yelling at my brother for hitting me in the head with a golf club. That spark made me think I was special because even though I was only three, I thought it was profoundly cool that I could see stars. I just thought that seeing these beautiful colors and getting my brother in trouble all at the same time were profound, even though I did not know what to do with that.

As I look back over all the times in my life like that, where I should have not survived, it makes me realize that there was a plan in place and that I was following the story line to the conclusion. We all have moments where the sparks bring about a clear directional change especially when looked at from a distance. Did life begin at these sparks? What if that event did not happen? Would it have changed the story line so much that life would have taken a drastic change, or would another event take its place? I find it all fascinating, mainly because I can look at the journey from a place of wisdom and see the ball moving through the pinball machine, bouncing off the different rubber bumpers, creating light sparks and heading in a different direction.

Another story that comes to mind in when my oldest son was driving home one icy and perfectly clear night. He hit black ice, and his car flew off the road, down an embankment, and flipped on its side. Dad to the rescue, right? Not really. I did call the tow truck, and we waited by the side of the road until they came. Standing there and taking in the crime scene shown on so many television shows, I realized that it was physically impossible for that truck to end up the way it did without intervention and without a scratch on my son, other than being shook up. I knew right then that divine intervention caused his being saved in his story line so he could go on to accomplish his spark.

If you have a family, you could probably pick out stories like this for each of your kids that were turning points in each of their lives whether good or bad in remembering their own sparks in time. My point is this: Did life start at that event, or did it just add to the drama of allowing the Spirit to play out in these vehicles we call bodies? We sure do put these bodies through a lot to try to determine when life begins and ends. But the most powerful point is that life does not end really, so all this spark bouncing off the bumpers is just a means to get to an end. You are going to get to the end and finish the game one way or the other.

No one can say whether your spark bouncing off the bumper was right or wrong. Only you, in your spiritual body and connection to the Source, can and should have a say in whether that was a right bounce or not. Yes, folks around you can try to affect the direction of the ball, but they ultimately don't have a say in your story. I recently read "I am not a body ... I am Spirit." When you put your daily movement forward in this context and when questions come up you turn to this thought, it opens a whole new way of looking at things.

I wish I would have figured this out prior to having put myself through so many bounces. It would have been a lot less painful. But you are right; it would have been a whole lot less interesting.

Enjoy the bounces and set your sights on the end of the game.

Green-Eyed Lady

Let me take you back to 1972. Imagine three college friends, of which I was one sitting in the dining room at school, which we did a lot of, and playing "Green-Eyed Lady" by Sugarloaf on the jukebox ad nauseam. We were all journalism students and part of the school paper, and for some strange but beautiful conjunction of energy, we all loved this song. Unfortunately, those around us were subjected to our required listening. We never gave them any other choice.

Flash-forward to me sitting at my desk in my current office listening to Pandora, and you guessed it, this song came on and stopped me in my tracks. It was flashback central. I was teleported to the smelly guy table in college listening to the beat, words, and rhythm of so long ago and smelling the smells, sensing the light, and feeling the feelings of that environment. Heck what was that? I mean, really, I now have kids a lot older than that nineteen-year-old I was at the time. During our lives, we all have memories, triggered by a spontaneous sight, sound, or feeling, that transport us to times and places—a subconscious memory. It can be good or bad, but I believe that the trigger is intentional and is bringing the memory up to help you either heal something or help you spread a message about something. I want to believe that this experience meant that my youth was not all bad and that I could be part of something like journalism, which at the time I thought was a dead-end, and not know where in the world I was heading while trying to understand why Green-Eyed Lady should be so important.

I believe that there are no coincidences, and all the things that we experience in our younger years, even though we may not understand them at the time, point to something in the future. Look at your life and see if that is true.

Oh, and just in case you do not think things like this lead somewhere, guess what color eyes my wife has sometimes? She is one of the people that seem to have different eye color based on mood and feelings. What do you think—premonition? Think about the possibilities. What if everything you have done really is a path and it really is the goal of the universe to gently direct you? I choose to not only believe this theory but also know that I am still on the directed path, and it is leading somewhere. Enjoy the journey.

Synchronicity

*One thing happens,
another comes along
without much thought,
they both tie together.*

*Things happen for a reason,
not by chance.
There are no coincidences
if you just relax and look.*

*Pay attention to what is happening
around and through you.
Don't let anyone tell you
that synchronicity is a dream.*

Chapter 2

FEAR

Let Spirit Bring You Home

It's the ninth inning, two outs, and I am at the plate with a count of three balls and two strikes. I fouled off four straight balls all over the place. I can tell I am wearing the pitcher out because he has that worried look, or maybe it is just him thinking that this guy can't seem to hit it straight.

I lived this event both in life and in my dreams. It feels very familiar to me because life has a way of making you think sometimes that you are at the end of the game and wondering whether you are going to win or not.

So, because I have access to an Archangel, I asked to have a discussion with Archangel Raphael, so I could ask him a question of such profound importance that I was surprised that I have not asked it before. The question was, "How do I get out this game successfully, feel like I have won, and try not to have a big ego about the results?" This resulted in the following discussion:

Raphael: *Strength is brought to you through making decisions. Going in and tugging on your cord with me and saying, "Hey, I need you in this moment to make decisions that grant me grace yes, but also strength, for I am ready to step up into more light, into my holy purpose, and into my consideration of faith." For faith is active, not passive. Your faith needs to be active.*

Mike: So, it appears to me that I bring conditions to my faith and that I need to see results and can't just know something will happen. That would explain why I try in my own way to pray for help or guidance.

Raphael: *Your faith is active, and therefore, at times, those prayers are so hard for you. For you cannot just pray and whistle along the way. No, that is not your truth, for you need movement. So, praying as you are walking is good, right? That movement facilitates not only prayers of faith for you but also movement of elements, like being out in the wind, or where water is running is a great time to pray for you.*

Mike: What kind of prayers are we talking about?

Chapter 2 - FEAR

Raphael: *These are prayers of faith, not prayers of I want or I need. Prayers of faith are saying I am ready to be one with you, Holy Spirit. I am letting go of all the stuff that seems to be crumbling around me and I am asking you to make the decision first, so I can follow your dots of awareness and accomplish my divine blueprint.*

Mike: I always thought that as a human I had to be in control and rely on myself to make the decisions and follow my created dots. But what you are saying is it is okay to ask for help and allow you to show me the way through your suggestions and that the dots if followed will lead me to my divine blueprint. That is brilliant.

Raphael: *When you feel stuck, move or put your feet in running water, stand in front of a fan, go take a shower, and have the elements of Earth move with your voice, move with your mind, and move with your emotions to create strength. Yes, the dots will come, and you will accomplish what you need.*

Mike: It sounds so easy to allow decisions to come through you so that I can be at peace with the direction that is placed in front of me through my faith. But my humanness gets in the way, and I worry about things like striking out and losing the game.

Raphael: *Your life right now is about cultivating you to be able to present the information that we share with clarity, with love, and with holy respect for the source and the nourishment that is for you and others when you give your life fully to us. You are part of me and in this holy placement our strength together conquers the darkness, heals the pain, and rewrites the thoughts that made the darkness in the first place. So, thank you for joining me on this journey of love.*

I felt like I had been told that the game was not as hard as I was making it. In fact, I imagined that the game was rigged in a way.

Whatever your definition of the Holy Spirit is, I see all the players being on the same team and trying to help you. No matter what issues press your life as a human, you can always turn to Archangel Raphael and his team with your questions about decisions, and they will help guide you by creating dots that you can follow. Archangel Raphael has said many times to call on him, but he also has said that you can call on your own Angels, and Guides. Human issues seem so trivial when put into the context of the divine. You always make it home, one way or the other.

Oh, and in that real baseball game, I did finally hit a double and win the game, or was that in my dream? It doesn't really matter when you have a friend helping you run the bases.

Everyone can feel a connection of some kind to their own sources whether it is their Guardian Angels, or guides by just understanding that being open to the possibilities, it creates a connection that wisdom can be attained to help them in their life. My suggestion is to reach out and communicate with whatever gives you the most comfort. What else do you have to lose?

Being Okay Now

"I am okay now." I would not have made that statement five years ago. But I have come to realize that I have stepped into a different age of reason. I won't place blame on age because anyone could say that it is a natural consequence of aging when you get to the point where you feel like you have done what you came for. I am talking about a much deeper spiritual development of under-standing that is like crossing a threshold into a room that, until now, I did not have the key to. This room is filled with relief and love of self in the understanding that I have accomplished something by being here. This can only be described as a sense that, in my first life, I came to help the souls set sail on their own journeys. Their mother and I had the honor of directing traffic, so to speak, and at least point them in a direction so they can all journey with those they find along the way. Attending my middle son's wedding without their mother as she had already died, brought a lot of introspection and made me realize that I really was put in the role of directing journeys, and at that moment I was okay with that.

So, enter stage right into a whole new story that I could call "Loving Again." I am lucky enough to realize that love does not have to end and that it can continue, albeit in a different format.

My come-to-Jesus moment was realizing that there are no rules. You do not have to save the world as a parent and direct traffic so tightly that no one ever gets hurt. It is okay to have an enlightened moment in the sun while watching a dragonfly buzz around you. And in that moment, it is okay to acknowledge that, no matter what happens, going forward in the time left in this incarnation, you did the best you could for everyone around you, whether or not a difference was really made. You only must answer one question to yourself: "Do I feel good about what I did?" If you can at least answer this question, you know you are in the right room at this point on the space–time continuum.

Being there for a child is probably the hardest thing that a parent can do because it is not normal in the ego-driven world to allow him or her to reflect that deeply. So, being able to answer that question for myself was important, and I now know that I had a purpose in both stages of my life and that, no matter what transpires, I made a difference to the only person in this illusion that I can really impact anyway—me. But I do know that, along the way, love was shared and that a difference was made. Now if I could hogtie my ego which is always trying to tell me that I am not good enough or that I am making the wrong decisions, maybe I could figure out a way of realizing that I do have wisdom and that I am okay, and can share that with those in my life.

     I wish for you that you have an illuminated moment and know that you are okay. Walk toward the threshold and open the door. You might be surprised what is on the other side.

Stepping into the Light

*Stepping into the light
from the darkness,
takes great courage.*

*Leaving the conditioned
responses behind,
creates fear
that runs deep.*

*Knowing that correct choices
came from bravery,
does not appease the doubt.*

*Accepting that faith
requires moving forward
without fully understanding
the direction,
means you understand
the journey has rewards.*

Chapter 2 - FEAR

Believing that Spirit will be there
to steady your walk
into the light,
will prove that you never
needed to be fearful
and that following
the path before you
leads you home.

Life Lessons

Sitting in the dark at five in the morning is a great time to reflect before movement takes place within the household. I seem to wake up early sometimes, like my father always did, just to sit in this quiet time. I always thought my father was silly sitting at the dining table doing his crossword puzzle and sipping coffee at that time of day. But isn't it funny what memory I have chosen for remembering him? The very images that I thought I would never find value in I end up doing.

I have been reminded that fruit does not fall far from the tree. Many times, I have thought or said, "I do not want to do this or that like my father." Yet, just by the very act of thinking or saying that, I now know that I was drawing the experience closer to me. It was not my not wanting the experience, but the laws of the Universe that were working in the background, just doing the things that they do. By putting my focus on what I did not want, I brought it to me all the same. So, my remembering my father at the table so early in the morning is just a small example of a powerful law that invites reflection so early in the morning.

When I was preparing for a surgery that my father also had, which turned out to be heredity at its best, I realized once again that stepping out from under the memories, pictures, and influences of the past is really hard. I think I realized that I ultimately wanted to be more like my father than I would have liked to admit. I could have done without the copycat surgery, but it did bring the opportunity for great reflection. I loved and respected my father so much that I was willing to follow in his footsteps and called to me things that would normally not be wanted because of the value I place on love.

Now I realize that I would like to remember him without taking on his energy, literally. A lesson learned about the Law of Attraction at this stage of my life will hopefully prevent me from any other truly hard lessons. The lesson I learned is knowing when to not give memories too much power. Enjoy the mental images, but keep them there and do not drag them kicking and screaming into your new reality.

Miffdom

All my life I thought that my mother had made up the word *miff*, because I never heard this word outside of my house when I was growing up. She was English, and I just thought that it was just another quaint word that I was used to hearing around the house. When I was recently in a less-than-good mood, "being miffed" instantly came to mind. Thanks, Mom.

I thought about ignoring the thought but decided instead to recognize that I was miffed about something. For some strange reason while in my miffdom, I decided to list all the things that made me miffed that day. Let's just say that the list was longer than I thought it would be. I was miffed about my income, my expenses, my job, the lack of a response from Spirit, my sleep deprivation, and my kids, among other things—you know, basically everything in life that isn't necessarily going the way you want it to. I think I had just hit my maximum miffdom ceiling.

That morning Archangel Raphael gave Trisha and I a quote: "Become aware of your actions today. What is fueling your actions? Is it love? Is it fear? Love and fear are the only powers of your reality."

Of course, everyone who reads Raphael's quotes thinks that he is talking to them. But this seemed like a direct communication to me. Remember, I said I was miffed about the lack of a response from Spirit. After that, I walked through the park behind my house with the dog, Jack, and to avoid another dog confrontation in one direction, I told Jack we should take a different path. So, I turned around, and in front of me was a path that I had never seen before. I have been walking through this park for thirty years, and I swear I felt like I was looking at something that I had never seen. It startled me so much that I entertained the idea that I was in a different park or that I was having some sort of senior moment. After all, I am in my sixties now, and maybe I was entering some unknown space that only maturity can take you to. When I came to my senses, I decided that what was happening was that I was being given a new perspective because I was just whining about it and Spirit wanted to make sure that I was paying attention.

The moral of this story? Create an action plan:
1. Make a "Miff" list.
2. Open your eyes.
3. Take a different path.
4. Accept that you are being watched over.
5. Be open to a new perspective.
6. Act in love and know that love is fueling your actions.

The Jump Rope of My Life

Sometimes I wonder what being fully connected to Spirit in a way that I would know by the feeling in my heart, the hearing in my ears, the knowing in my mind, or the seeing with my eyes is like. I know that these are just intuitive markers, and I completely understand that to connect to Spirit, you must choose to communicate in a way that sometimes is unbelievable. My faith guides my direction, but my impatience sprinkles roadblocks in my path in a way that even though I know the process I find myself doubting my own reality.

We are all surrounded by Spirit all the time, but we usually don't pay attention to it or we get so caught up in the conditioned reflexes of our past that we don't open ourselves to the possibilities offered to us. Take me, for instance. Ever since I have been on the Spiritual journey, I have come to believe that all I must do is connect the dots placed in front of me. I have seen so many miracles that I have lost track of them. I just know that the path ahead is guided by love and forgiveness and that, in the short time I have in this form, I can accomplish good things. But like so many around the world we must live in this space, and it is so hard to turn off the ego that keeps telling me to not risk and that whatever I am thinking probably won't work out.

So, how does one stay on the path, so to speak, without sounding like a Spiritual zealot? I think it is easier than we think. If we could just set aside our doubts and trust that the connections placed in front of us are valid and are without a doubt perfect for us at any given point in time, then we would know that we are in control of our own illusion. I have been speaking with Archangel Raphael for the past several years and truly do love this connection. It has created a healing in myself as well as a business of delivering his messages, which I love. Recently I had felt a disconnect of sorts from Archangel

Raphael, which was unprecedented in our relationship. I was always able to communicate with him when I needed to, and it gave me a strength that I can only describe as comforting. But over time I had felt his pulling away from me, but I didn't know why. Had I done something to piss off an Archangel?

I was able to discuss this with him in a channeling session, and to my relief, he told me that he was pulling away a little because the time had come to send me in a direction that not only included my work with Trisha and him but also a new connection to another source that would fulfill my destiny. He said that he has been there for me in healing and would continue to stay with Trisha and me, with the goal of getting his messages out to the world. But the new source for me was the messenger of communication and would create a whole other direction to help me achieve my own path with Spirit. Here I thought that Archangel Raphael was my only mission, which I was perfectly happy with. He said that he would never let go of me and that he was holding one end of the jump rope while my new Spiritual source was holding the other end. He said nothing is separated and we are all part of the same energy field. Wow.

I believe we all have this capability to interact to Spirit in a way that is beneficial for all. I don't know what is going to happen tomorrow or the next day or year, any more than anyone else, but I do know that, like myself, we all have the potential of being on the journey if we just open our hearts and listen, see, feel, and know that without faith and an open mind toward the possibilities that exist, we risk that love and light will not be seen, even though it is always around us.

I have no idea how this new added dimension of my life will transpire and even how to start. But when you have an Angel telling you something after all these years, ignoring him is hard. I am happy to be on this journey no matter what it looks like and look forward to this new Spiritual source. I welcome him or her with open arms and, as always, will find everything fascinating. So, bring it on. My lesson to pass on is that doors open and close and you never know what is on the other side of the door, but if you follow your heart and truly listen, you will find yourself on a new adventure that will always be rewarding. If nothing else, you will know that the jump rope is never abandoned, and you can count on support from both ends. Thank you, my friends.

I Am on Your Team

Letting go and falling into the arms of Source without the constraints of fear sounds easy enough, but how many of us talk a good story about doing just that but are worried about the fall and really wonder whether we will be caught? It is not really unlike being on a sports team where you have confidence in who you are playing with so much so that you are willing to let your fear of losing be tossed into the wind and go with the faith that you are with the perfect group, the perfect mission, and the perfect time to win. Not everyone gets to have the feeling of winning, but people divest themselves of the fear that they won't win. You must do this to have enough confidence to take the step toward working with a group that takes you out of your comfort zone.

 It is like that with Spirit. If you believe that we are all one, then it does not stretch the imagination to say that we are all on the same team. You cannot see the team necessarily but if you really believe and allow the feeling to enter your space, you will know without a shadow of a doubt that there is more out there then maybe you were willing to consider.

 As far as the fear of falling and whether you will be caught or not, what have you got to lose? Some people just know, some feel, some hear, and some see, but for most of us, we must take it on faith that there is a place we fall to and that there is a guarantee we will be caught.

 I have decided that no matter what happens going forward, I know that I am on a much bigger team than I could have ever imagined. I always liked playing first base when I was younger. I don't really know if it was because I oversaw an area on the field or if I just liked being in the action and having things thrown at me to let me know I was alive, but I can say that I trusted those teammates without really understanding why. I just look at it now as being on a bigger team. I have Angels playing other positions, family members watching over and cheering for me, and a safety net made up of the Source I choose to believe in ready to catch me if I trip and fall or if I decide that the journey is over.

Think about the powerful image of your own team as you round the bases. Even if you don't see anyone on the field. Just knowing that there is a team can make life so much easier to accept and help you relax. In moments of strife, fear, anxiety, and just concern in this ego-driven world, this image, when focused on, brings me back to the freedom of running the bases, the crowd cheering, and the wind blowing in my hair to reach home plate, and me yelling, "Dang right, I am on your team as long as you want me. Thank you for this great game."

To Know

Go to that place,
where it feels right.

Go to that place
where the tingles
continue long after the event.

Go to that place of wonder
where you were always told
it was your imagination.

To know,
is to accept the energy
that you were given to feel
long before you came.

To know is to allow yourself
the grace of being who you were
suppose to be and
who you want to be.

The Thread of Love

The thread of love, the thread of love, the thread of love—okay already. I heard you the first time.

This very distinct string of words kept popping in my head, and like all the other times this has happened, I had to write it down, because "they" wouldn't leave me alone until I did. "They" are—you guessed it—my Guides, friends, Angels, acquaintances, or maybe just my subconscious. It really doesn't matter because what I have learned is that when something is stuck in my head, I need to write it down and think about it. I have been thinking about it quite a bit. I am reminded of the first time that I met Archangel Raphael.

Having never seen a channeling session before, I must tell you that I was frozen in my seat but totally fascinated at the same time. What I got out of that first meeting was that he loved me and that his message is all about love. In fact, pretty much everything he says through his Facebook messages, monthly presentations, videos, and books is about love in some capacity. Yes, he will talk about various subjects, but if you really listen to the messages, through love, he almost always brings you back to it.

One time, to help Trisha become less fearful about the process, he told her that she was just channeling love. He gave me an assignment once that required me to come up with a three-word sentence to describe our relationship with him. "Love Is Enough" was the answer. Perfect. So, everything that is handed down to us and that we pass along to others through ourselves or through our business of passing along messages is all about love and light. If we can stay in that field of reasoning and not act in fear, then the "Thread of Love" will be sewn throughout everything we say and do.

The thought of passing along the true meaning of why we are all here makes me feel that I really do have a purpose in life that goes beyond the mundane of daily living. I, for one, plan to hold onto that thread with every cell of my body. The visualization of an unbroken thread connecting all past events with a connection all the way back to the Source being handed to me is quite a picture. If love truly is the thread connecting all, then I accept the responsibility of not breaking that thread on my watch. After all, I would not want to be the person responsible for breaking the thread of love.

How about you?

My Reasons for Being Here

Does wanting something make it so? According to the Law of Attraction this is a true statement especially if you put your feelings behind it. I was told recently that my Life Purpose "was to come as a passionate person and to participate in time and space. This passion makes you comb the beaches of all expressions to find those nuggets that will make a difference for all of humanity. You seek for all so in passion; your voice and your words become the bricks that build structures of truth through experience so others can feel and be sheltered, to be nourished and understand that they, too, have placement of purpose in love. Your voice is just beginning this path to give others color in eternity." This was just an excerpt from Archangel Raphael's Life Purpose reading of me when I requested to be the guinea pig for the new Life Purpose messages. I am usually the first to stand in line and to hold my hand up when it comes to new things.

The first time that he gave a message on Life Purpose and talked about the different categories that we choose to come with each life and make our main purpose, it resonated so deeply that I made fun of him and said that he was just creating a new book for me to work on. He just laughed and said that there was so much more. I immediately saw the importance of this Life Purpose message. All my life I have always thought that there had to be more and there had to be a reason for me that went beyond just living. I could never put my finger on it, but I knew that I wanted to give to humanity something that means something more than what fast-food place I am going to eat at.

Purpose to me gives me a foundation to work with and matches up to my whole life's story of knowing that there had to be more to being here on this wonderful blue planet. Growing up while my father was in the Air Force, seeing poverty around the world; knowing that I would adopt children, play baseball and swim; knowing that I was okay with being average; wondering like all kids what feelings for girls was all about; knowing that I would someday be part of a profound nuclear family with so many different wants and likes of their own; and knowing that I really was never in charge of them and was only participating with them in their journeys still led me to believe that there was something missing.

Archangel Raphael simply explained Life Purpose this way: "we are here as no accident, but part of a holy design co-created with the Holy Spirit to bring love of all to the anchor of creation with all elements within the human form which we hold as your holy temple of awareness. Part of the structure that you have created is to come to lives with a Life Purpose that will erase the patterns of karmic pain forever." By describing the different Life Purposes that we all have chosen, he has allowed me to finally be at peace with what I came to do. Now, of course, the proof is in the details, and it is up to us to get to the end, but for me, just knowing that I had chosen a purpose for being here, and seeing how much it fits me, renews my spirit and fills me with optimism again.

We all have a purpose. How important is that? Talk about enlightening. Just to know that you can not only see your purpose, but you can use the information to heal that karmic pain that tends to trip you up life after life.

I plan to use this new knowledge to stay on course and try to live up to my own reason for coming. I might as well work on the things that my soul thought was important enough to make it a priority in deciding to come this time. If nothing else, I have the passion and want to answer the question of whether wanting something makes it so.

FAITH

> Depending on the religion **faith** is belief in a god or gods or in the doctrines or teachings of the religion. Informal usage of faith can be quite broad, including trust or belief without proof, and "faith" is often used as a substitute for "hope," "trust" or "belief". Some critics of faith have argued that faith is opposed to reason. In contrast, some advocates of faith argue that the proper domain of faith concerns questions which cannot be settled by evidence.

> This is exemplified by attitudes about the future, which (by definition) has not yet occurred.
>
> —Wikipedia

I want to talk about "faith." For several reasons, faith has been on my mind, and because I think that most of the time, if I have the issue in my mind, then maybe others do too. We are all connected as one at the God or molecular level, depending on whether you are coming from the spiritual or scientific point of reference. I don't think it matters which focus you come from because we can all talk about faith. We all have it in some form or the other. The argument that I was having with myself about faith seemed to be divided into two camps. There is fear-based faith and light- or love-based faith.

Fear-based faith takes me on a journey of wondering why things don't happen when I expect them to. Being afraid that the choices I make aren't going to lead to the outcomes that I thought when I made those choices, mixed with a strong ego, is truly an awe-inspiring adventure into the poor-me syndrome. Maybe I don't have enough faith to pull it off, or maybe no one is listening, and my faith is falling on deaf ears. You can see how the spiral down goes. Trying to figure out how to maintain the level of energy needed to keep the fear-based faith from driving you crazy is exhausting.

The other side of the argument told me that all I must do is love, project it, and have the faith that things will work out exactly as the universe wants it to work out. Let me tell you that although this form of faith is easier and less stressful, it takes a lot of confidence in yourself and whatever you believe in to maintain that air of exuberance. Being somewhat of a doubting Thomas that deep down really wants the proof shown to him, I find that this easier version of faith really stretches my thinking in all directions. I do love the feeling of this version of faith, though. It has a calmness that is full-bodied, and if you have ever been in deep meditation, it is like that.

Even as I write this, I know in my heart that the love and light version of faith is the right way to go. A great friend of mine once said, "What do you need right now?" He was telling me to go with the well-lit path because it is much easier and not hung up on negativity and self-doubt. I think I am going to try harder to have faith in the universe, to believe in me and in my connections. To have faith in what I know is right and good and to take a chill pill when things aren't necessarily going the way I want because you know what—I don't know what is behind door number two anymore than you do. But my faith will make that *Let's Make a Deal* prize just right for me.

Have faith for a better tomorrow. Believe in yourself and the outcome will be perfect.

Resetting the Grandfather Clock

What do you do when an Angel tells you to go on vacation and focus on yourself? Do you argue? No, of course not. This came about because I was not feeling connected to Spirit like I have in the past, and my internal talk was about poor me. I really do have funny conversations with myself, but I figure I am the one who understands the importance of listening to Mike. The feeling of the lack of connection made me think about how I do normally connect. Asking Spirit a question and getting some form of response that allows me to relax and know that I am being listened to at a high level is just natural.

There have been times in the past when I felt disconnected, but this time seemed different. What I realized was that as much as I talk about following your heart and staying grounded, a time comes when the proverbial floor drops out from underneath us and we are floundering like a fish. But, why do we have to go through that when, in fact, we are never disconnected? All it takes is a request to have Spirit participate with us and it will.

When I sat back, focused on my heart Chakra, and grounded, the feelings immediately came back. You know what I am talking about: the energy surge, the tingling around the Chakra, the flow of what I can only call love emanating from a place that I picture are free from the daily grind of the human condition—all come at the same time. It reminds me that I am never alone and how little it takes to connect to Source in a way that is meaningful to me. It is almost like resetting a grandfather clock that I knew as a kid. You had to pull the chains to create the energy to turn everything back on. But over time, the clock runs down and must be reminded that it has energy to share with everyone.

So, when an Angel told me to go on vacation, go camping with your dog at places unknown when you haven't been camping for thirty years, what did I do? My first thought was, "Are you crazy? My old body can't do that anymore." But that energy thing creeping over your body has a strange way to make you see things differently. As I headed out with the dog, with the hope that we would survive, my sense is that communication with Spirit will truly happen in the form of nature, writing my thoughts and meeting people along the way.

I would like to say that I will never go down that disconnected slide again, but I know that is too idealistic because we humans really can't maintain any level of functionality consistently for an extended time. In my humanness, I accept that I will have ups and downs in the future, but I will try to remember that help is always there and that all we must do is ask. Somehow that alone makes me feel at peace. We need only remember the asking.

My guess is that there might be some interesting stories that come out of this trip, and secretly I do hope to connect in a powerful way, but if that doesn't happen, I will keep trying. Who knows, maybe I will finally see that UFO — hint, hint.

Acceptance

Acceptance to me now is not as bad a word as I thought it was when I was younger. Maturity has a way of rounding off the edges of words that you thought you would not necessarily use to describe yourself as you age.

I recently had to accept the fact that I couldn't do things that, when I was young, I didn't give a second thought to doing. Hiking in the remote eastern Oregon wilderness with my oldest son had been a wish of both of us for a long time. I had my shoes, water, camera, bugspray, and sunblock. The only thing I forgot to bring with me was the courage that I guess I left at the Grand Canyon when I was young and did not mind sitting on the edge to take pictures. It had made my wife nervous, but back then I was invincible, and that it could be dangerous never crossed my mind. Compare that to my hike along, what I would consider, a goat trail with a sheer drop of two hundred feet down on one side and a mountain on the other side, I realized very quickly that I wish I still had that courage as I sat on the trail, overcome with fear that prevented me from getting up and moving again.

What do you do when that happens? Of course, I called in the Angel squad to come in, calm me down, and help me to breathe as I realized that I was holding my breath. It would have been comical except for the fact that my son's dog kept acting concerned and returning to me with encouragement.

I must tell you that in moments of crises, the Angels do come through. They surrounded me with their energy, got my breathing under control, and basically told me that everything was going to be okay; that, yes, I wasn't twenty anymore; and that maybe I should consider that *acceptance* should be my watchword as I move forward. I was not going to argue with them hanging on to that trail, but it did give me something to think about from that point on.

Acceptance is not a negative word to me anymore, and I am proud to say that I learned my lesson well, as the next day of hiking brought a trail that was only a mile long but straight up, and halfway up, when I could no longer fill up

Chapter 2 - FEAR

my lungs with air, I sat in the shade and said that I accept that I can't do it.

I think acceptance is hard as we age, but, in my mind, it was a great lesson in limitations that I will use over the rest of my life. I encourage everyone to accept who they are and know that the Angels really do step in when you ask for help. You may not like the new limits, but reality has a way of opening your eyes and making you pay attention so you can be here for years to come with your family. You can also hold out for a new family story—the day your son tried to kill you off!—and a lesson on acceptance for all the generations. Enjoy the trail.

Chapter 3

RISK

The Bird Party

Winter comes in with unexpected surprises some-times. Take, for example, a moment of reflection I had in my office while I looked out the window at an empty birdbath. Not only had it recently frozen from the cold snap; it now sat empty of all water as well. Birds flew in and stepped around looking for water, and then, I swear, they looked over at me in what I took as a bird glare that gave me the feeling that I was not doing my job. So, I thought about what should I do—because bird glares are not pretty.

Of course, I immediately took a pitcher of water out, filled the birdbath, and went back to work. A few minutes later when I looked up, I saw twenty birds having a party at the birdbath. It was like they had called out to the neighborhood that there was this guy willing to fall under their mind control and give them what they wanted. It could have been like a creepy movie, but I felt that there were deeper lessons here:

1. You do not stop giving just because the climate changes.
2. The little things do matter.
3. Love given freely is all the reward needed.
4. Big birds chase little birds out of the abundance.
5. Some share better than others.
6. All sentient beings enjoy a party.
7. When the party is over, everyone leaves.
8. Be happy in your heart that you are able to participate in the party.
9. Paying attention to those around you and seeing what you can give are not bad things.

Free yourself from the bonds of what should, could, or must happen and follow your heart to the answer. Find peace in knowing that you have the answers if you are willing to listen and see the birds take flight.

I Am the Angel . . . You Are the Angel

Thinking through all the snapshots in my life where danger was imminent, I realized that I could not figure out how I survived a lot of times.

Chapter 3 - RISK

As a kid, I jumped at the sight of a centipede by my hand and fell backward into a crevice in the desert. The fall was probably ten feet, but I should have been battered by the walls I was shooting past. Instead, when I came to my senses, I was sitting upright atop a boulder at the bottom of the crevice—without a scratch. I do remember thinking it odd, but being a Boy Scout at the time, I just wrote it off as I was a fine specimen of a rugged outdoorsman.

Reviewing my mental notes, I realized this has happened a few times and has made me recently connect the dots. I started thinking about Angels coming to the rescue at various times in one's life and how they do it. With all my personal work on oneness, it suddenly occurred to me that when crises happen, we subconsciously reach out for help; because we are all one, we are calling out to ourselves.

Just think about it. If you believe in this illusion, then who are you really calling out to? If my Guardian Angel and I are one, then aren't I just asking myself to save my butt? I mean who better to save me than me? And when the time comes that I can't save myself, then I just get to go on a great trip back to the oneness. I think I really like this idea of being the Angel for myself and not putting the burden on a Guardian Angel who probably has better things to do than look after me. But just in case, I will hope the A-team is there as backup for me. The options are always good.

Sometimes thinking deeply can give you a headache. In this case, it feels like my heart is lighting up, which tells me there is something to this being-your-own-Angel gig. Listen to your heart song and see how it feels for you.

The Hand of God

"The Hand of God" can also be referred to as an act of God or as events outside of human control, such as floods or other natural disasters, which insurance companies love to use this definition so they can get out of paying claims. Isn't saying that no one can be held responsible just another way to place blame on things that we don't understand?

I think it sad that humans place blame so easily on what, for all intents and purposes, could be classified as Spirit. It is so easy to place blame somewhere else when we really create our world, and all results attached to it. Take, for example, global warming. Everyone has an opinion, and there are different, very polarized camps on the subject. Some say it is manmade, some say it is an act of God, and still others say it does not exist. Why does it matter when the result will be the same? No water is no water. Why not just accept the fact that something is happening and as a collective do something about it?

In duality, the ego plays such an important role that you don't know what is happening until you go home and review. I would love nothing better than to flip a switch, light up everyone's aha button, and have everyone simultaneously get it. But, of course, I am just projecting my wants and beliefs on everyone else, and that takes away free choice. Man, this stuff is complicated. I guess the real answer is that humanity either figures it out in time or it doesn't. If you can step back and realize that we all probably end up in the same place anyway, no matter what decisions we make, then life on this planet does happen because of the hand of God, especially if you subscribe to us being one with God. So, here I am once again at the beginning and blaming myself, Spirit, God, or you for whatever I feel I don't have control over. Works for me. Good luck, Mother Earth.

So, where does that leave all of us? How can we apply this concept that says that something is happening without being interfered by all the different opinions, dogmas, and political arguments? How about we all just agree that water is important, that we want water for our children and their children. Just the act of agreeing that water is important will combine all of our energies into the oneness of thought and by doing that one act, it will bring consensus into the mass consciousness through the energy of combined thought. It really is that easy. And then over time mysteriously solutions will be found, and you can look back and feel that you input your energy into the solution.

The Case for Being Naïve

Being naïve has its merits. It can protect you when those around you are maybe thinking that you are nuts: "Why in the world would he take that on just to fail? It will be so painful and probably is not worth the effort." Can't you just hear it, or have you felt it before?

In retrospect, I do not know how many times in my life I was so naïve that I didn't even know I was. Throughout my life, even if I did not know I was doing it, I set goals of things that I wanted to accomplish without a care in the world about how hard it might be or whether it would be successful.

Recently I was reminded about this as Trisha and I were nearing completion of our intuition book. Looking back to when that first came into my focus, I realize I was so naïve that I did not know what I did not know. Somehow that makes sense to me. If I did know what I did not know, I might not have taken that first step toward publication. And that would have been a darn shame because at my age, I would have missed so much about the journey and all the steps that go into at least learning about what it takes to get a book from an idea to a published book that you can hold in your hands. What a trip.

This reminds me of another naïve period in my life. As I mentioned, Barbara and I had six kids, of which three were adopted. I am sure that each time we adopted another child, people whispered that we must be crazy or that it was going to kill us, if not drain all our resources. How many times have you thought that when you've seen a big family? Again, for us, being naïve was a great vehicle for moving us forward through the incredible process of helping a child obtain a new life. But what is mostly missing from this conversation is the fact that I am a better person for it. I learned so much about love, forgiveness, sharing, caring, and growing during the many years the kids grew up together that I consider it my legacy.

So, what lessons can be learned from being naïve?
1. Being naïve leads to passion.
2. It makes you not consider all the supposed facts.
3. It places a Spiritual bubble around you where you know you are being hugged and pushed forward.
4. It brings joy to your life because whether you achieve anything or not, you are trying.
5. It brings things into the world through manifestation that did not exist before.

6. It extends your life through the many people that you touch along the way of trying to accomplish the goal.
7. It helps you to not get stuck in the mud so to speak because you are afraid to risk.
8. It brings the sun out when the forecast said it was going to rain all day and you were prepared to get soaked on your walk.
9. It plants seeds in your mind, soul, and body that being naïve is a great way to tackle new projects because you can accomplish anything.
10. Most important, it can make you a better person than you thought you deserved to be.

If you cannot already tell, I am a big fan of being naïve. At least in my own short life on this planet, I have accomplished so much more because of it. Now I know that we are not all the same. We have different personalities, risk tolerances, and fears. But my suggestion is to be naïve and take the risks in life that, when you look back, could prove to be the most important events that ever happened to you. What do you have to lose, except all that mud on your shoes because you have been stuck for too long?

Be the naïve soul that Spirit wants you to be and let it hug you and help lead you down the path. Enjoy.

Freefalling into a New Story

Freedom lights within and without and cannot be swayed unless you use your fear-based response to impede its flow. Everyone struggles to make the journey flow smoothly, but humans have a way of creating potholes that interfere with the straightness of the road. True freedom is there for everyone to enjoy and use to their own betterment or of those around them. People struggle to make the way home fit their own perception of reality, and it is all well and good, but just remember that you are making it all up. Why not make something up that reflects a picture that has smooth, straight roads? You can take control of this picture by realizing that your story is just that—a story. Writing a different ending to your story is okay. Reach into your mind, which never truly dies; touch all those past life experiences; and stop repeating the old stories. The universe with the help of our friends the Angels will be glad to help you move past those repetitive dreams and experiences that affect your movement forward into this lifetime. Do not be afraid to ask for help. They only wait for the opportunity to help you remember what you are running from and give you help and direction to connect the dots. When connected, these dots will bring joy and enlightenment to your world and will create a whole different pattern of behavior that, when reflected on, was always there for you to access.

Letting go and free-falling into Spirit can be scary because you do not know if someone will be there to catch you or whether you will just continually fall. Letting go has brought clarity to my life and trust in something other than the stories that humans make up. Free-falling into Spirit is not turning yourself over to another dogma but creating the freedom for you to finally give your mind the opportunity to risk and create with love and feel the energy of the Soul that you have maybe never felt before. You will think more clearly and will suddenly find that you have been connecting the dots all along. Colors will become brighter, the people you look at will look back at you, and you will carry yourself differently and breathe the air of freedom for maybe the first time in your life.

Your whole life has brought you to this moment in time right now, right here, for a purpose. What you decide is your purpose will affect everything going forward. Take the time to get in contact with the real you through whatever means makes you happy and feel the energy flow and ask for divine truth. You will get an answer if you are willing to risk and listen. Now you can compare and make a decision based on the options you might have not had before. Enjoy the moment and know it has always been there. Putting things into perspective gives you the freedom to make choices on what you want, not on what stories are being placed on you. Move forward with clarity and a feeling the Angels are there to catch you and help you connect the dots. Human success is only in the eye of the beholder. What matters most is how you feel about your own purpose and whether you see yourself driving down a straight, smooth road.

One Hand to Another

I recently attended a convention in Denver, and I came away with one thing: homelessness is universal. I spent ten days on the road, and no matter what city I visited, homeless people wandered the streets at all hours. This is a reflection on the times and the lack of attention to the fact that, as a whole, our moral compass has changed positions.

I remember being in Panama in the sixties, and even as a child, it struck me that the poor didn't deserve what they were living in. I knew that I couldn't do anything about it, but it didn't stop me from feeling that my privilege made me somehow feel bad.

Even today when I see all the homeless everywhere, I still feel that my privilege does not feel right even though, like so many, I am sometimes one paycheck away from being in their shoes. I am sure that in a past life I have been in this situation many times and that is why my feelings seem so raw.

So, what do we do about this? How do we go about changing our moral compass to point in the direction of bringing humanity to the world? It is a huge undertaking and seems so big and overwhelming that it can be thought that one person can't really make a difference especially in a political climate so filled with unsettling issues. But that is the point. One person can make a difference—one at a time. Why can't we somehow set a goal for each one of us helping one person a year? If I help someone and you help someone and everyone in this world of turmoil helps one person, then the problem will be solved. I know it's easier said than done. But this straightening of our moral compass must start somewhere. Why not here? Why not now?

People and families can become homeless in so many ways, and the reasons don't really matter when you think about it from a Spiritual direction. Their plight may have been predesigned to serve a purpose. What I know is that my journey here included empathy and was meant for me to learn love in so many ways that when I return home, I can say that I made a difference. I am choosing to reach out to one person this year to help.

What about you?

Chapter 3 - RISK

Floating Down the River of Life

In the course of being human, we want to take the safe route, which, by all means, only makes common sense. But common sense doesn't necessarily fit into the realm of Spirit and intuition. Many times, we find that we can't make sense of what is going on around us unless we just fall into the energy field and go with the flow, so to speak. So how do we create a safe route and still allow ourselves to feel Spirit and connect with our own intuition?

When I was a kid in Arizona, when school was out and we were free to be kids, we sometimes went tubing down the Salt River. This was an all-day affair that consisted of leaving a car at the end of the run and driving everyone up to the start in another. Then we would float down the river all day. Now, this was not necessarily a safe route. The river was cold at times, there were things in the river, and oh, the typical desert animals were hanging around. And it always produced a great sunburn, as well as a lingering aftereffect. Even when not in the river, a day later, I always felt like I was still in the inner tube and floating. To this day, I can still remember the sensations of floating.

To me, falling into energy meant that I allowed myself to relax into what I thought at the time was wanting to be in a group. But, looking back, I knew that I was being watched over and wouldn't come to any harm. This was a feeling of being connected to something that I couldn't explain. As a kid, I had no common sense, and having to rely on something else that I couldn't describe or necessarily even sense was awkward but real all the same. Taking the safe route would mean that I never did anything, and for a kid, that, of course, wasn't going to happen. So with the help of the unknown, I took risks all the time, sensing that something more was going to automatically help me when I needed it. This is certainly not common sense, but don't we all have the sense that there is something more, but we just cannot put our fingers on it?

As adults, we are supposed to know better because of all our life experience. But I believe that most adults are just like those kids always trying to take the safe route. We sometimes sense that there is more, and because of our so-called life experiences, we do have more proof that there is something beyond our understanding of what being human means. Most of us, however, never connect it to Spirit or intuition, so we go through life never really feeling the connection. Only after we move on through death do we find out that we could have been safe and felt the connection to Spirit at the same time. If only we would have the remembrance throughout our lives that Spirit is always there to help guide us whether we know it or not.

So common sense really is something that humans all have the capability to access through their feelings. My contention is that if we just open to the possibilities that Spirit is in our lives, we can always access it, and we can apply it to all our movement in this world, then there would be no risk and we would have common senses with all there is. Opening up to the common senses shared by all, and with Spirit, will truly create a much safer environment for us to live in. Enjoy opening up now so your future self can relax into a world of amazing possibilities.

Reaching Out to Risk

What are you afraid of? It seems to me that we spend most of our time here worrying about what might happen and never acting on the thought causing the fear instead of taking the risk and stepping into the unknown energy source by being the creator. The traditional bell curve places most of humanity somewhere in the middle of the risk curve. Then the rest are divided between those that never risk and those that risk all the time.

I must admit that for most of my life, I was safely within the confines of the middle with most everyone else. Then I took a chance on Spirit and find myself risking all the time. It is not right or wrong but just a divergence from the norm. Maybe the older you get, the safer you feel from risk fluctuation, or some form of brain-freezing takes over and you do not particularly worry about what others think.

That was me as I have stepped into the world of Spirit, especially over the last five years. Not only have I given permission to myself to fall into the arms of the "wholly Spirit," but I have also enjoyed the most fascinating journey along the way. So now, it turned into a risk fest because I have stepped into Spirit which is outside the norm of the bell curve for most people. But under it all, I know that I am being hugged and just need to ask for help when I think I am being overwhelmed. I believe that Spirit can only help us when we are receptive and ask for help. Risk is just an avenue to an unknown that, with the help from our friends on the other side, does not have to be scary but can be the best thing that has ever happened to us.

My guess is that I always had that risk tolerance, but I felt safe in the middle. Sometimes it takes an event of extreme emotional significance to push you out of the nest to see if you are going to flap your arms fast enough or reach out to something different as you fall. Lucky for me, I not only reached out but also found myself holding onto a very strong branch that let me down easy. It in no way makes the path simple, but it means that there is more to life than just staying in the middle of the risk bell curve. It means that there are options we do not know about and will never know about unless we reach out for something that is beyond our sight.

What are you willing to risk finding out?

Midlife to Cool

What do you get when you put a sixty-two-year-old on a brand-new red motorcycle? I know you are thinking—midlife crises, right? I prefer to call it midlife cool. Midlife crises always bothered me until I saw that the life expectancy is headed toward 120. So, now I think I am just acting like a thirty-year-old who needed an extra ride. No big deal, right?

Little does the rest of the world know that even though I look cool on the motorcycle, I am not remotely secure in my skills. I'm just going with the flow and faking it till I make it.

I think our relationship with Spirit is like that. Most of the time, we believe that we can master the relationship. But, really, we are just hoping we don't crash and burn. We talk about the relationship, but sometimes we just know that we are faking it till we make it.

But, just like learning to do something new like riding a motorcycle, age has nothing to do with it. Your belief and faith do. Feel the air on your face, see your completed journey, know that everything turns out, and keep your ears open just in case a siren is sounding behind you or you really do hear that still small voice talking to you.

Enjoy the journey, keep your eyes on the direction you are going, and don't forget to wave at the others that go by who look cool also. Live your joy.

Skating to Freedom

Picture a skater on a completely flat, frozen pond. This thought occurred to me as I was talking to someone about their life and how it has become easy for them as they have achieved their goal. This person was not happy with their performance and felt that they are just skating by because they achieved the goal they wanted. The problem with that thinking is that you can become complacent in your actions, trying to stay on the flat ice and hoping nothing upsets the flow. I think we all get in this safety mode and forget that life has its bumps as well as its ups and downs. Speaking for myself, I can say that I have skated for the past years in the hope I could get to that smooth part of the pond.

Talking to someone else about skating through their life and not taking on the bigger challenges, I realized I, too, have been skating through life and not taking the bigger challenges on—an aha moment. I think that at my age, I sometimes think that I should be able to sit back and take it easy. The problem with that is life has another idea. The other thing I realized is that because I was skating through life, I had lost the personality that had made me successful in the past. This new view of skating up and down the valleys of life allowed me to remember who I was and to pick up the pieces of me that I could use going forward.

Are you just skating by because you find it easier, or can you take on new challenges that will allow you to skate to freedom?

Hanging Out in Life

Would you risk your safety to do a job that most people would think was crazy? No, probably not. What is risk anyway? Isn't it just something that takes you out of your comfort zone, challenging your senses to do something that just doesn't feel right? I contend that risk is just a challenge that takes us down a different path or trains us to do something that we never thought we could do. Risk is only negative until we get comfortable within ourselves, and through conditioning, it becomes rote and therefore not risky.

I happened to be downtown, sitting in the sun and enjoying the afternoon. I kept hearing noises and couldn't figure out where it was coming from until I looked up about four stories. Two window cleaners were hanging from two ropes apiece, swinging back and forth and just chatting away without a care in the world. My first thought was "Holy crap! Those guys are risking so much." I would never do something like that. Just watching them scared me. But as I watched, that they enjoyed their jobs was obvious, and it put me at ease somehow that there was not as much risk involved as I thought there was.

I contend that risk is inherent in life. Just think about the first time you rode a bike. I rest my case. For those of us in the light-and-love arena, risk is big at first: What are people going to think? Do I tell my family? Do I pretend that I am "normal" except when I go to a crystal-and-rock store or when I peruse the Spiritual bookshelves at the local bookstore? Risk is no different in our regular lives than in our spiritual lives. No matter what religion, spiritual direction, or beliefs you have, you still risk what other people think about you. As humans, that seems important to most of us. But risk is placed in our lives to make things interesting and to challenge us to reach out and touch something new. We shouldn't be afraid of showing that we are willing to risk in whatever our beliefs are.

Being like the window cleaners, feeling comfortable in their job, leads me to believe that risk is not necessarily good or bad. Just our reaction counts. Being honest in our risks creates opportunities to expand into areas that need our light, and if nothing else, they might give us a thrill.

Jack's Passion

Passion is defined as a strong and barely controllable emotion and an intense desire or enthusiasm for something. *Passion* defined the essence I knew as Jack. Granted he had some unusual passions but loved to share them with anyone around. For instance, he loved food, snow, and little animals and just loved harder than anyone I know. When we met on the newly powdered snowfields, I just couldn't help but watch his excitement as he proceeded to turn himself white from his total absorption into that cold world. Seeing him love something so much became infectious, and I found myself running and diving into the snow myself, with total disregard of the looks we might be getting from those walking by. Food, I must admit, is not my passion, but when Jack was with me or a group, he would demand trying everything—including what was on your plate. He had no care in the world about what it might look like, and in normal settings it might be a turn-off, but with my friend Jack, everyone thought it was cute. As a side note, my God, Jack could attract women. I wouldn't say I was jealous, but I was amazed by how easy it was for him. How some can be so good at that special kind of attention is amazing.

Most of us struggle to stay within the confines of what is considered proper. My English mother was always in the back of my mind telling me how to present myself to people. Not Jack. He didn't care about what other people thought. I often wondered what it would be like to just act the way I wanted, like Jack, and not be subjected to the thoughts of conditioned influences. Wow. Love abounded with Jack in his love for little animals. He just couldn't help himself. His passion drove him to want to hug every little animal that he could get close to. It was fun to watch him try to get close to animals around him. He would talk to them, run in enthusiastic fun, and skip in synchronicity with the beat of nature, always aware that his friends were watching him and wondering if committal was needed for his passion.

But one day as I was spending the day with Jack, I realized that life was short, for no other reason than I was almost run over by a car, which left me in that oh-my-God awareness that life as we know it can take a quick turn and have you miss the opportunity to just live. I remember Jack looking at me, and I think he said, "See, it can happen fast . . . How does that make you feel?" After seeing my life flash before me and having my heart start again, I looked at him and said, "You're right. I want to be like you. You have infectious passion about almost everything and you don't fall prey to the voices in your head about what you should and shouldn't do. I want to run and jump in the snow, have women notice I exist, eat all types of food and suffer the consequences, and love little animals. Life is short, and I want passion in my life."

That is the lesson my friend Jack gave me while he was alive. Yes, unfortunately Jack died from what probably was a bite from one of those little animals he loved so much. Infection can happen fast and shorten our lives, but we can all live like him in passion for life and love and spread that to those around us. I no longer take life for granted. Like Jack, I look at life with the knowledge that life is to live with passion about things we care about no matter what family or friends think. After all, our contracts with this existence not only brought us here but is also giving us permission and the source energy to use this passion to live like Jack—with excitement, love, and commitment.

In case you did not know or didn't guess, Jack was a dog. He loved every day with complete and absolute passion. He loved the snow, food, and chasing little animals. I know that he would not have wanted it any different. He taught me lessons of love that I can never fully thank him enough but can only hope to emulate in the rest of my life. I am not sure I will ever be quite as good at life as he was, but I can try. And

I think that is the lesson for all of us. We can try. We can love things that don't necessarily make sense, we can step out of our comfort zones, and we don't have to worry about what others might think.

Live life like Jack. Thanks, my friend.

Look Up and Change Your Conditioning

When you can't see the forest for the trees, my experience is that you are not looking hard enough. When on a hike in eastern Oregon recently I was focusing on putting one foot in front of the other to not embarrass myself by falling, so I was not looking around until we came to the top of an incline and the outrageous beauty of a meadow with a vast variety of alpine flowers nearly knocked me off my feet. This is a literal interpretation because the flowers were so thick I tripped over the vines.

How is it possible that an expanse of wilderness can be so beautiful when a week before I was immersed in "normal" life with the electronics of the world blaring fake news and there is so much concern about the next big threat? I want to say that I let it happen and forgot that beauty in nature is everywhere. But I, like so many, am conditioned to the world we live in, so much so that we forget that another world beckons us to new Spiritual heights if only we would look up and over the rise in the trail and get back to what Mother Nature is begging us to see, if for no other reason than to pay attention. My theory is that Mother Nature places beautiful things in front of us not only to entice us away from all the other distractions, but she is also saying to look closely and see the minute details of my beauty. Seeing the amazing intricate designs in all the flowers when you are sitting down in a meadow of color that goes on forever is quite extraordinary. Moments like wandering in a sea of wild-flowers so thick you must guess where the trail is puts humbleness into this human form.

      Don't forget. Look up as you walk through life and see what is real and allow your conditioning to change. Who knows, if enough of us look up, we may be able to save this planet after all. And if you cannot go hiking in an alpine meadow and walk through the flowers, then just go to your neighbor's house and walk through their flowers for five minutes. Just don't tell them where you got the idea.

The Hallelujah Experience

      Have you ever thrown common sense out the window and proceeded with something you wanted "come hell or high water," as my mother used to say? Of course, you have. Part of the human condition is proceeding even if our common sense or Spirit says, "Whoa big guy. You might want to think about that." This recently happened to me even though I knew that I always have access to Spirit and can ask questions and more than likely get a response as to whether proceeding is smart or not. I of course did not do that.

My daughter and I wanted to spend some time together, so we met at an agreed-on destination to go hiking. Great idea. It would be a lot of fun, and we could create great and lasting memories. So, we set out in the morning to our place of conquest in Utah that included a visit to a slot canyon that I had never seen in person. The problem was that on that day, the temperature soared to 108 degrees, and did I mention that it was mostly hiking in the open in a very dry, unforgiving environment? It is funny that when you start out on a hike in the morning, when it is cooler, you forget that you must turn around and come back. Oh, did I mention that I had my dog with me also?

So, as we proceed through the first two miles, the thought comes to mind that this slot canyon thing better be worth it because so far, the sand and some of the beautiful cliffs rising up above us were nice, but at the same time we don't see any other people, so I had the sinking suspicion that maybe the people back at the parking lot just wanted to use the restroom and that they weren't going anywhere near that trail. But we proceeded with naivete and determination, which meant that we have come this far, so we darn well won't turn around before we see something spectacular. I was thinking this as the dog was running back and forth between the shaded spots—a definite hint.

We finally came to what looked like a narrowing of the valley we are walking through, and as the "Hallelujah Chorus" suddenly played in my head, we entered the slot canyon, which I can only describe as one of the most beautiful things I have ever seen. As a photographer, I ran around in the cool shadows of this canyon amazed by the light coming through the upper reaches and illuminating the twisted red walls in a way that you would think that what you were seeing could not possibly be real.

After getting our fill of that glorious light show, we realized that we had to walk back the way we came, and the temperature had risen 10 degrees from when we started. Needless to say, we all moved from shade to shade—if there was any, poured the last of our water on our heads, and made it back to the world of the living. Let me tell you, heat exhaustion is very real.

Big lesson to this story is that if you follow your common sense all the time, you might not see or do things that do require some risk but can lead to possibly some of the most profound moments of your life. Spirit is always there to guide us but at the same time to protect us. So, use your common sense, of course, but don't let it control your every movement to the detriment of awesome experiences.

Chapter 4

EGO

The Basics Are Good Enough

Go into any of the stores that change your car's oil and you get blitzed by all kinds of questions and statements: "Your oil is dark, and you need to clean it." "Your air filter looks like it has been through a war zone." And, of course, there's usually the mention of the dreaded metal filings in the transmission fluid. These people are good, but they keep hitting on you until you cave or say no.

It is kind of like ego, and as we go through our daily lives, we are bombarded by it trying to tell us what we should or shouldn't be doing. It is exhausting at times, and to a point, you tend to just cave in and go along with that little voice in your head. It sometimes seems easier to just go along than to stand up and say no. As I was going through the oil change process the other day, I took control for some reason and said no to all the bombarding questions and statements coming at me. You know what? It felt good. Not only did I realize that there was more than one way, but it was also not the end of the world to say no. It doesn't really care about anything except trying to control what you do. To keep this ego from taking over, I think sticking to the basics of Spirit helps: listening to your heart, living in love, accepting no pain story, finding that moderation is a good strategy, and looking for the truth in all that you do. What is your truth, and what basics can you use to help you weight the demands of ego? Going forward, I will be challenging myself to take a breath before major decisions and reflect on these basics to determine if it is ego or truly my heart talking.

You are each placed in situations where you have to determine who is in control. Put thought into whether you are using the basics of Spirit to control your life or whether you want ego to issue the decisions. It is ultimately up to you, but from what I have learned in my spiritual quest, wouldn't you feel more freedom if you are calling the shots? Let's all put ego in a little box on the shelf and revel in the freedom together.

Seeing Differently

Remember when you were growing up and you wanted to do something so bad that you worked at it until it drove you crazy? I remember it took me six months of constant effort to try to learn to whistle—not just any whistle, mind you, but whistling by cupping my hands together and blowing through my thumbs. For the life of me, I cannot remember why I thought this was so important; I just knew that I had to reach that goal or that I would forever have a headache from trying. Having grown up and realized that childish wants were just that, I know that I was applying the same need when wanting to learn how to view auras.

    I consider myself to be an average person who simply finds everything fascinating, and when I want to do something, I read and read and read and practice a whole lot. Sound familiar? Occasionally I would get glimpses and get excited about the possibilities. But I never thought I was getting anywhere beyond the simple things that you see.

    Then, as if by magic, one simple lesson in intuitive skills, which took less than thirty seconds, gave me a very simple change in my method and opened a whole new world. What I discovered is that by relaxing and letting go, and by not trying so hard, the door opened, and then I could not turn it off. It was, of course, there the whole time, which is the interesting part of life. We make a change so hard, yet if we just relax and fall into the change, it usually works out just fine.

To this day, I can whistle, although there is not a big call for it. Once you accept the change needed, relax in the flow, enjoy the journey, and have fun, you can do anything, and it becomes a permanent part of your new makeup. This is an example of ego at work and in my case blowing so hard in trying to whistle that it would give me a headache, or focusing so hard to see energy around people, when in reality it is much easier to do. I just told my ego to knock it off and chose to look at the problems differently. I guess my mind gave up trying to block what it thought I needed and allowed me to see differently.

If change is hard for you, why not look at it in a different way? Relax into it and go with the flow, but most of all, enjoy yourself and have fun.

A Lesson from the Child on the Roof

A small child climbs a fence and climbs up on the roof of his house to watch massive rolling thunder- and dust storms headed toward his house in Arizona. Spirit says this child's fascination with wind is great. The child thinks that at some deep level, the storm is moving ideas and feeling around the world, and he wants to be in its path and flow in the direction that it is going. Ego, on the other hand, is yelling in his ear to get off the roof before something terrible happens.

It reminds him that nothing good comes from something he can't see. So, just before the storm hits his house, the child gives into ego's concern and gets down. And so it goes for this child throughout his life. He wants to flow with Spirit, but ego keeps him chained, so to speak, to safety.

Fast-forward to today and, you guessed it, I was that child. I still watch the wind in the trees, listen to the wind chimes, and wonder what is traveling around the world in the wind. The only difference for me now is that I am making a conscious decision to stay on the roof and stand in the wind. I do not need to see what Spirit is trying to direct me to, and I am no longer afraid of the consequences. I guess that is what age will do to you. I can tell my ego to take a hike and send its controlling thoughts back into Spirit's white light to be recycled into something that feels better.

Thumbing your nose at ego's controlling thoughts and breathing in what I consider to be Spirit's mission statement to all of us here, which is love and forgiveness, are quite freeing. If we could only teach this to our children when they are young, just think what improvements they would make in the world. My challenge to you is to think about what your own definition of Spirit and ego are. If you could eliminate something right now that you know is ego-based and holding you back, what would it be? Create a meditation for yourself. Breathe in your picture of Spirit, hold it, and let it settle throughout your body, and then breathe out the ego-based control, such as lack, pain, fear, inadequacy, or any other one that you want to get rid of. This process for me has been life-changing because I know that I am giving up all those things that really aren't important and am attracting what I really came here to remember.

Try it. What have you got to lose? Help the child on the roof in your life flow with Spirit and find a little more meaning to this ego-filled world.

Held by the Confines of Ego

Shining bright within the confines of your form is a heart that beats to keep you alive. But according to Archangel Raphael you live without your heart in Spirit, where there is no need for the form that we come to love and hate. Duality is like that. You really can't win sometimes, or at least you don't think you can win. If there ever was a time to touch the meaning behind the heart, it is now. But the ego drills deep within your psyche to let you know that you rely on this heart to live. It repeatedly tells you that you can't live without the heart, so don't even try to separate yourself from the strings attached to this life.

But what if you stand up for yourself and reject the ego's endless prodding? Do you immediately turn into mush and get condemned to whatever you have been told? I think not. Knowing that you never really die but live on in Spirit forever should bring comfort and a realization that you are being fed a bill of goods by the ego, which, at the same time, loosens its hold on you.

Most people on this planet do not allow themselves to think outside of this ego box that has them so controlled. That is okay because we each must follow our own journey of awakening and realizing that turning away from ego's grip brings comfort and choice to work with Spirit of our own choosing. Being enlightened is just that: waking up. All the stuff going on around us all the time is just so darned confusing and stepping away from the requirements of what we thought was our reason for being here opens a door to a new place that few take advantage of.

The most important person you need to be here for is you. That is not selfish or shouldn't make you feel guilty in any way. What it means is that if you do not take care of yourself and establish your core meaning at the Soul level, then you are just doomed to repeat things over and over. Breaking away from the pack, so to speak, and understanding the meaning for you first are the best ways to then be able to help those around you to wake themselves up. And guess what? When enough people have woken up and it becomes a movement that can't be stopped, the promise from

Archangel Raphael is that we will all fall away from the dream in front of us.

Being of sound mind does not mean that things are clear. It means that all our minds are connected at the basic level of Spirit and that we can communicate at the mind level just by our thoughts. We can love one another and encourage everyone's movement to waking up and being enlightened, and most important, opening ourselves to there being more to life than just doing, being, owning, and living within that ego box where the ego tells us that only he can help us.

Here is what I feel: Step away from ego's incessant voice and feel the connection to Spirit however that looks and know that Spirit is waiting to lead you back and away from the need to feel that you are separated from the oneness that we truly are. So, when you hear that still small voice, then maybe you should listen to it.

Around Sound

Dissolve salt in water and what do you get, besides the obvious: saltwater? While I was mixing salt and water to treat a sore. It reminded me of Spirit. Salt seemingly dis-appearing into the water, but it is still there. It was a beautiful illustration for me as I was asking myself where Spirit was. Of course, the answer seems too simple. Spirit is right in front of me, in me, around me and part of me. In other words, to use a phrase that has been coming up in our intuition class, it is in full "around sound." There is no place that Spirit isn't, and when I started pondering the deepness of that, it made for quite an argument among my mind, my ego, and my desire to see, hear, feel, and know Spirit in a more intimate way. My desire would be to have any Spirit take a chair and talk to me like my days in journalism during college. How difficult could it be really? Just think of the articles that I could write from that. But I know it is more complicated than that. Just because I have the desire does not mean it is going to happen, especially while the ego fights to protect me from myself. It is interesting how such a simple thing as dissolving salt in water can turn into such a deep reflection. My new desire is to try to figure out how to see the other "crystals" in life that I intuitively know are there and put my ego in the closet, so it won't prevent me from participating with Spirit. I would ask that Spirit try harder and maybe meet me in the middle, so I can prevent myself from trying so hard. Okay, I get it. It is really about the journey. Who says salt is not good for you? Pass the salt, please.

Sending Guilt Packing

What is guilt? Is it the connection to an unseen force that makes you react in ways that you don't understand, or is it a tool to be used to help you take stock in a moment in time and reflect on where you have been and where you are going? Being a Cancer, I have always known that one of my lots in life was having guilt ingrained in my soul. Ever since I can remember, I felt guilty about one thing or another, and I must say it did make me a nervous child. I think all of us feel guilt at various times in our lives. Some more than others. I was from the "some more" camp. And when you get married and have children, at least for me, the issue was just compounded because there is so much in a marriage that you just want to make right. And you either figure it out in a way that is peaceful, or you end up splitting because you can't fulfill that force of guilt within your psyche.

It is too bad that we can't come into our lives knowing that guilt is a tried-and-true instrument of torture that the wonderful character called ego is so well trained in and provides you the opportunity to really take on that role. After all, the ego's primary role is to always keep you off balance, and what better way than to use guilt as its tool of choice.

Here is what I say to ego: "Get lost! I do not need your help anymore in accentuating my guilt complex. I am no longer a child who can be manipulated by your control, and I choose differently." Of course, this is easier said than done.

The ego is strong in its wish to control your survival. But there is hope. Just by recognizing that there is a better way and that you do not have to allow the ego and its minions to control you opens a new door that leads you to think differently. I now understand that I have more control over my thoughts than what I thought. Knowing this forty years ago would have been nice, but better late than never. I enjoy telling my ego where to get off and feeling the release in my body. The trick is to remember that you have the right and the ability to reject the guilt cloud that ego likes to place over you. The physical release that you get from understanding this and letting go of guilt can be so cathartic.

You are probably wondering what to replace guilt with. The obvious answer is love. It is not a hard stretch of the imagination that if ego is controlling guilt, then love is the opposite and is being controlled by you. Connect to something more meaningful and know that this is one of the major lessons to be learned in any incarnation. The next time you feel guilty about anything, remember that ego is controlling the puppet strings, and choose to tell that darned ego to take a hike. Immediately think of the most powerful force in life. Ask love to enter instead and feel it in your physical form. Enjoy the right that Spirt has given you and remember one of the reasons why you are here. So, the next time I feel guilty I am going to try to remember this lesson and use my Spirit given right to shoot guilt down with love.

Eventually, the subconscious will take it in and it will become second nature. This shift to love will change your life.

Raccoon Metaphor

It does not happen consistently that a moment in time so influences my mind that I must go write about it. Okay, maybe it happens more than I realize. But I think that most people do not see events because they are not tuned to a certain reality or frequency. Let me just lay out this scene.

Minding my own business while on a long walk through town, as I approached a four-way stop, out of the corner of my eye, I noticed movement coming down the sidewalk to my left. My mind said, "Cat," but my eyes told me something else. It turns out it was a raccoon limping down the sidewalk. He looked like he has just come in from a night on the town and didn't realize how ragged he looks. (I say "he" because I was not about to check.) We reached the corner at the same time and casually stared at each other, as if this happened every day. I could see he was really hurt, and I went into my save-the-child routine by looking at my phone and realizing I did not know who to call. I told him I wanted to help if I could figure out who to call. He just looked at me and, apparently, decided rescue wasn't going to happen. He

Chapter 4 - EGO

wandered across the street to a neighbor's yard, trying to get away from the crazy dude telling him it would be okay.

I finally decided to call the city, and they said they would send someone. In the meantime, my new friend was ticking off the local dog and showing teeth I believe were from an alien. Waiting for the city personnel to show up and retrieve my new friend, it suddenly dawned on me that my Puritan ethic of saving him was probably going to get him killed. So, one part of me said let him go his own way and find peace or not. The last vision I had of my new friend after I told him I was not going to interfere with his life was of him wandering down the street to who knows where under his own power to an unknown destiny.

Now, that this experience, although very surreal, meant something is not lost on me. My take is that our roles as family members, friends, and co-workers can sometimes be construed to make us think that we must take on the role of savior. We must save them despite their own willpower. Helping them cross the street so to speak without getting hit. Although helping people with love and advice is a correct course of action, forgetting that self-determination is a prime directive of being here on this planet made me realize that my new friend had the right to choose the direction no matter how messy he looked. Remembering this lesson allowed me to walk away while knowing that no matter what happens in the raccoon's life or my family's, friends', and co-workers' lives, it is right and perfect. May you find help along the way without losing your ability to determine your own journey.

Why

*Why is it that when you can't find love,
it is staring you in the face?*

*Why is it when you need an answer,
you don't hear it being whispered to you?*

*Why is it that when fear takes hold,
love is hiding in the mist?*

*Why is that when pain takes over,
it is allowed a voice?*

*Why is it when you see a miracle,
it can't be seen for what it is?*

Life

Let the Guitar Sleep

Santana wrote the line "while my guitar gently sleeps." I thought about that line for fifty years on and off, of course. I knew it had some meaning to me; I could feel it. I just didn't know how to interpret the feelings. Having had some training in intuition I now know that I have feelings that can be understood through a whole set of sensory sources that I never knew I had. So, of course, I had not figured it out until now because we, the males of the species, don't typically know how to get to those innermost thoughts easily because we are usually to surface-oriented or just wrong. I don't mean for that to sound harsh, but reality bites sometimes. Women are good at digging deep and feeling at a level that only confuses men, so much so that no matter how much we try to enter the conversation, we usually are only thought of as trying to come up with a solution to whatever the problem is on the spur of the moment to quell the obvious tension in the room. I admit it. I really don't want to think too deep because it usually hurts my head, and I get caught in the inevitable damned-if-you-do, damned-if-you-don't moment. Now, don't get me wrong; I am a nice guy, and I do deep down think that I should be smart enough to fix anything at any moment, at least that is what my ego tells me. In reality, I don't know squat and should always be in the apologetic mode of behavior even if most of the time I don't know what I am in trouble for. See, a man without a clue.

But there is hope for me and other men. We need to stand up and admit that we do have feelings that are not unlike a skimboard flying across the surface of the water. Yes, stand up and admit that we have thoughts about what it would be like to feel the pain in childbirth or the moment when your teenager turns away from you and says he or she doesn't need your help. And I will prove it to you. This Santana line means a lot of things to me now compared to the days when I used to play in a band, Crystal Violet, and thought he just turned his guitar off. So, that is depth, right?

Anyway, back to feelings. This Santana line has several meanings for me:

1. I will stop playing my guitar while you share what is happening with your favorite TV program, meaning that I will listen even though I may not have any clue what the heck is going on.
2. I will quiet my enthusiasm for whatever sports event is going on and create something for us to do together. With reruns in today's world, it doesn't matter anymore.
3. I will turn down my thoughts to something more than the race-car mode and enjoy life a little.

4. Most important, I will stay in touch with those spiritually inspired intuitive locations that I never knew existed and feel my way back into understanding the deeper meaning behind things when it comes to being the best friend, best partner both in business and life, and best spouse that I can possibly be given all the limitations that I and society place on me.

I believe it is okay for men to feel and to express those feelings in the right moment, of course. That is the trick. Timing is everything. That lesson will come at some later date when I understand it myself. The point is that spiritual development through training in intuition, or whatever modality, can give us so many more opportunities to feel beyond what we normally see and hear. I believe that, offered with love, these feelings can produce a better person, let alone a better environment to work within. It doesn't mean that it will be perfect. Feelings have good and bad effects, but honesty creates a union within which results will be generated to keep you on the appropriate path.

My advice is to touch real feelings through your spiritual practice, however that looks, and enjoy the freedom that comes from letting go of holding in the dysfunctional nature of surface feelings. Relax and let the guitar sleep.

Chapter 4 - EGO

Things Happen

Within the confines of a life we meander through the ups and downs while trying to control everything that happens. This is perfectly normal. Throughout history, humans have tried to leave their imprint on things to feel in control. The problem is that we find out that things happen that we have no control over. Why is this? I think that if we have chosen to be here in this incarnation, we should be able to control everything to our satisfaction. This, of course, is narrow ego thinking. We have been lulled into thinking that we can and should control everything, including behavior, love, world events, other countries, and ideas, among others.

Part of waking up is realizing that controlling everything is not sustainable and shouldn't be because when unexpected, and maybe unwelcome, things happen, it is the opportunity for enlightenment. I can give you an example. When I was about three years old, the first memory that I have is being hit in the temple with a golf club swung by my older brother. I should have been seriously injured, but other than seeing stars, what I absolutely remember is that even at that age, I understood that things I have no control over happen. I didn't choose to get hit; it just happened. But I can look back on that scene and I see everything so clearly, including the weather, the grass, the colors of clothes, and mostly the look on my father's face. The look of terror in his eyes of his second son nearly being killed was something I would never forget. But the point is that the knock in the head, as jarring as it was, was being seen through the eyes of a soul rather than a human that was not three years old. It was a very rational moment in which I knew that I was in a tiny body, but I was thinking, "Wow, I don't want that to happen again." I believe those moments shock the soul out of the human body, at least for a time, and gives you that connection to your divine self and, of course, to a life lesson that you will remember.

I can look back through many things that have happened over my life where the shock value of certain events put me in an immediate frame of mind that I know was not related to my age. Those split seconds almost seem to connect you to the soul that you really are.

I guess my mother was right. What doesn't kill you makes you stronger. What I would personally like is to connect with my soul in a little gentler way short of having to go through the pain of things. But we all must take it the way it comes. Controlling everything is not necessary. Just let things happen. I am guessing that they all work out in the long run anyway.

Chapter 5

GRIEF/FORGIVING

Leaves on the Forest Floor

I write these messages that in my mind come from a Spiritual or Angelic source or from my own musings from somewhere deep within my psyche. Wherever they come from, I do not try to distinguish their source necessarily, but feel the need to just write them down. Learning intuition has given me a framework to place around what happens in these inspirational moments. Six years ago, death entered my doorway with great fanfare and proceeded to lay siege to what probably in my mind was a "Leave It to Beaver" mentality. While I was raising a family, protected by the fog of the fifties, that things would ever change never occurred to me. You know that when you live in a dream, you make it up, so that is exactly what I did. No complaints here.

Then, in one fell swoop, the fog dispersed, so to speak, and opened a world I did not really want to know. This is what happens to everyone facing the death of someone they love. The stories are different, but the journey through the fog of delusion opens a doorway into creating a new you. Whether you like it or not, things will never be quite the same.

In my case, the event opened a world of inspired thought that, at the time, I could not even imagine where it was coming from. I did know that I had to do something with it to get it out of my head. I have come to discover that I was using some different senses that suddenly decided that the time was right to irritate the you-know-what out of me, but I was not in the frame of mind to fight anything. I just followed along like a puppet on a string because at the time, the only thing I did know was that it seemed to be in a forward motion.

So now, when I get these inspired thoughts based on one of the Clair-senses, I react in a much calmer and accepting way. Clair-senses are your intuitive understanding of the world around you. By feeling, knowing, hearing and seeing not with your physical body, but with your heightened intuitive senses, you can open a whole new world of understanding of what is going on around you. I write these thoughts down because usually I am excited that I am connected to Spirit in a way that seems to work for me. That is where the title of this message comes from. I was walking through the forest, and guess what? Things slowed down, and I acted like I had never seen leaves on the forest floor before. It is funny how that works. Because of my increasing knowledge of the Clair-senses, I knew I was looking at these leaves from a different perspective. The message to me was that they float down and create layer upon layer, covering what was once there, like life.

I think about my life and the layers upon layers of stories that have occurred over it. I am grateful for all of them, just like the leaves, that have floated down on my presence to help teach me that death and life are one and the same. Even though we sometimes think we are alone, these leaves bring their nutrients to us in ways we don't even understand. They help the soil to create an environment with just the right amount of everything needed to help growth. Leaves can sometimes just blow around you, and they can settle with the certainty that only they understand.

I have concluded that learning about intuition has allowed me to open myself to letting all the past, present, and future leaves in my life swirl around me and to being in the presence of inspired thought without giving it an earthly and ego-based name. Acceptance and faith are probably the keys to enjoying that not all things have to be named and that if I want to be inspired by leaves gathering in layers on the forest floor, then so be it. Enjoy those moments that you think aren't rational but for some reason make you think harder and deeper about something.

Talk to the Wind

*Talk to the wind,
ride the wave,
see where it goes and
who it will touch next.*

*It always answers
through its gentle pushing and
pulling of nature's gift to mankind.
Feel it against your skin and
be one with its flow.*

*Surprise yourself.
Open your heart.
Be with the friend that has always
been there and never expected anything
in return.*

*Allow the wind to take your thoughts
to other people and places.
Maybe they will listen and return
the thought someday.*

Lesson Learned

Every year come rain or shine, a special time creeps into my psyche. I don't ask for it, and it is not something that I put on my calendar. But it is real nonetheless, and I can count on its consistent request for me to notice.

Joshua Michael Russell was born in 1978 but held onto life for only ten days. But in those ten days, I became a human being with so much more potential than I would have ever guessed possible given a tragic event such as losing a son could hold. Only by looking back after so many years can I apply a deeper meaning to the death of a firstborn son. During the dramatic and profound crises, of course, survival is the only thing on everyone's minds, and at the time you, do not realize that the loss of someone so important could have anything redeemable to it.

But I am here to tell you that during the years since Josh's death, my occasionally thinking about the "what-if's" about him did create a bond with him. Of course, studying spiritual subjects over the ensuing years has created for me an understanding of our connection to Source and the sense that we really are all one and can never be separated. I have talked to Josh and walked the Oregon beaches asking for him to give me a sign of his presence. Yes, I know that it sounds like hanging on, but if we are all part of the same Holy Spirit soup, so to speak, then aren't we just talking to ourselves anyway? I have no guilt about communicating with everyone that I have loved in an open and accepting way with the expectation that they can hear me and can respond.

One day, I was thinking about Josh and wondering what life would have been like if he had not have been part of my life. The following life lessons occurred to me because I was touched by his Souls energy field:

1. I do not believe that we would have had all the kids we did without him because Josh touched us so profoundly in his short life that we wanted to give as many Souls a place to land as we could.
2. Maturity in my human form came very quickly after his passing. No longer could I stay attached to immaturity and the freedom of thinking that bad things do not happen. It gave me a kick-start into accepting and planning the future.
3. His death opened my heart even more than it was to depths and levels of love that I had never known. The births of my next three children were met with such profound love because of the lessons taught to me by this child that we had for such a short time. Each time a new baby was placed in my arms, I felt so connected to my past and my future. I felt that it was important

to pass along the simple love that was taught to me by this little soul called Josh.

4. Josh also promoted our deep need to give more than we had and ultimately led us to adopt three beautiful Korean children. If he could give us so much in ten days, why wouldn't we extend ourselves to others who needed a home?

5. Most important, Josh taught me the value of life and death and how little separation there is between them.

Because of a tiny little bundle of a human being as flawed as he was physically, I can't help but thank him for coming and sacrificing his future for a few days of love and for lessons that would last me a lifetime. I owe my parenthood, my career, my beliefs, and my beingness to having known him even if it was for such a short time. These lessons tell me that people come and go in all our lives, and although we may feel that it might not have meant much, all Souls touch us in one way or another. Everyone you have ever met passed some sort of energy to you; whether good or challenging, it has had an impact; and along with all energy from all people you have met along the way, the cumulative effect has resulted in the person you are today. None of us are an island.

So, thinking about one of the Souls that touched my life reminds me to thank everyone who has had input to the person that I recognize as me. Thank you so much, Josh, for seeing in me a reason to come to this planet to share and set me on a journey that has meant so much. And while I am at it, thank you to everyone in my life that has come in and gone out and left an imprint. I look forward to the new folks coming in whom I haven't met yet am anxious to see where the effects will take me.

What if you look back over your life and remember all of those that have touched you in one way or the other and realize that you are who you are because of input from many sources. Good and bad experiences have an impact and it is how you take those experiences and apply them to yourself that create your forward motion. It is not easy by any means, but it does have a way to put your life into perspective.

The Planned Journey

While going to the Oregon coast on one of my reflective journeys, I tripped over an aha moment about the Soul's purpose. No, I am not an expert on the Soul, but this moment seemed very clear to me in that I realized that we all have a reason in being here. I was thinking about the vivid pictures in my head of intense or specific moments in time during recent years that taken separately are just individual pictures. But putting these snapshots of events together created a full story surrounding my wife Barbara and her illness and subsequent death. I believe that at the Soul level, we come into this existence with a plan. We may not remember the plan, but we do carry it out over the time we are here. There is a plan founded in love, and we go on our merry way, moving toward the ultimate result.

In this case, I was able to put together different snapshots I wouldn't normally put together and fit them nicely into a story about someone who, at the Soul level, really knew what she was doing. Each step on her journey here was choreographed to perfection resulting in exactly what she wanted to complete. Now, of course, those left behind sometimes feel that it is too soon, or we take on a lot of guilt about the process. But at the Soul level, I find it remarkable that we come in with a plan, execute it, and go home with exactly what we need. When I realized that all the different pictures fit together so well into a complete story, I was amazed and humbled by her love of herself and control in carrying out such a beautiful story.

At the physical level, the story can look messy, but at the Soul level, it is incredible to think that we all are doing this very thing. We come in with a plan, carry it out in whatever format we think is best, and then leave to reunite with the one thing that puts everything into perspective. What a beautiful and brave undertaking for all of us to realize that we do have control and that if we would just take the time to really understand the meaning of the Soul's journey, maybe, it will make our visit here a little less awkward and a little more directed toward taking responsibility for how we interact with the rest of the Souls in this space. After all, the collective of Souls is all trying to accomplish the same thing that Barbara did, which was to finish the story on their own terms.

May your story fit together the way you have created it to, and may your family someday have their own aha moment on the beach of their own journey.

Seen It All

You may think you have seen it all, but you probably have not. You may think you have felt everything possible, have experienced all miracles, and know what is coming, but you are dreaming. How many times have you seen, heard, or felt something only to question its reality?

I believe we see little miracles all the time and are either conditioned to ignore them or told they are not possible. But I am telling you that things happen that we should not ignore, if only from the standpoint of accepting the possibilities that the Universe is trying to communicate with us.

Let me give you an example. Jack the dog had his favorite squeaky toy that looked like a hedgehog. I knew it was his favorite because he didn't tear it up. He carried it everywhere. He loved it and always seemed to know where it was. When he died, I was cleaning out things, and that one toy was not around. I assumed that it was lost in the yard under the bushes somewhere only to be found years from now. In fact, while I was walking, I made the comment that it was too bad it was lost and generally wondered where it had gone. I do not know if I was missing him or what, but when I walk, I tend to let my thoughts wander.

I got back to the house and was moving the laundry from the washing machine to the dryer—you can guess where this story is headed. Of course, right on top of the laundry was the hedgehog. To say I was shocked is an understatement. It had been weeks since Jack had died, and I can guarantee that it was not in the basket when I started the laundry, and no one was in the house at the time.

So, what do I have here? Could it be that at a time when I needed a reminder about the miracle of love, this hedgehog was given to me as a present and was proof that there is a connection between Spirit and humans? Could it be nothing more than just a little nudge that Spirit is really listening and that, when needed, it will give you a clue that was needed? Or am I dealing with a ghost dog who is going to haunt me with his hedgehog for the rest of my life?

I choose the latter because it makes me feel good, and it fits my sense of humor. Feelings are the key to unlocking the Law of Attraction, so I choose to live in the world of small or larger miracles and believe that if a little dog wants to make sure that I remember him and, at the same time, help me to believe that these connections exist, so be it.

I think that the hedgehogs of the world should unite and give us all those clues to Spirit's presence, so we do not get lost in our minds. So, for me, I keep questioning and looking for those momentary glimpses into an unknown I look forward to sharing. It is amazing what one little hedgehog can do to a psyche and body to regenerate a path of excitement toward a Life Purpose that I would like to fulfill. Thank you, Jack, for sending me the reminder that I am not just human and that there is a much bigger picture than what I can see. May your hedgehogs poke their heads out of the laundry and help you connect and bring you peace.

Saying Good-bye

I got the bright idea recently to write an article with Archangel Raphael mainly because I had just lost my longtime friend, Jack the dog, and during a channeling session, I was feeling sorry for myself and wanted to get Raphael's take on my loss, especially after he was talking about the ego game. I managed to express my thoughts on my ego saying that I did not do enough to save Jack, but my heart was saying that my love for that little dog was all that mattered and that I was not going to make him suffer anymore.

When you lose someone, whether human or not, at least in my experience, that darn ego talks to you and tells you that you are never good enough and that you should have done more. Then guilt sets in, and your weak, grieving self takes up the mantle of martyr. It is quite exhausting, and even though you want to fall into this weakened state of agreeing with the ego, it is good to be able to talk with an Archangel to help set you straight. I want to share with you because I cannot possibly be the only one on this planet to lose a dog that I thought of as human. So, I asked Raphael what he thought.

Raphael: A journey to support another before you is a relationship of, as within so without, for you and for them. This journey allows you to come to understand the questions, Are you love? Are you making the decision in your now with love? It is hard to fully define within your mind what love is.

Chapter 5 – GRIEF/FORGIVING

The construct of love is vast, and you just know tidbits that recognize the essence of love. When you are defining a decision, the ego loves to throw coins of identity at you, for these coins create a way to sell out your love and to sell out your decision in what you know is true in your love.

Mike: I was wondering at this point what coins we were talking about?

Raphael: Your world that you perceive has many coins of duality: the yin and the yang, the yes and the no, the win and the loss, the good and the bad. As you are sitting in your world right now, you are flipping these coins of value in the game of duality and worrying about what side of the coin will show up. Will it be abundance, financial loss, love, hate, home, homelessness, or life and death?

Mike: In my case, I was flipping the coin of whether Jack should suffer through hospitalization just to make me feel like I did everything possible or whether enough was enough and peace should prevail. That coin is a tough one because even though ego usually wins these games, at the time, my heart was closer to the finish line.

At the time I was using everything I could think of, including communicating with source, to try to achieve peace in a decision that I could live with. I wanted Raphael to expand on this thought.

Raphael: The ego throws decisions of magnitude through piggy banks upon piggy banks of coins holding pain and pleasure at you. Ego wants you to hear the tinkles of coins instead of the softness of love. Acknowledge major decisions and remember that we are hugging you always. The space really is more of love, for you cannot get out of it. It is hard to define love, yet it is what you seek, for it is eternal, and it is your birthright. When you insulate you with the Holy Spirit bringing the remembrance of absolute love even for a moment—a blink of a blink of a blink, that passage allows you to know the right decision. The ego's game is to keep throwing those coins at you, yes, even after your decision is done, for the ego wants you to play chance because it can keep you running. Spirit knows the permanence of love and knowing your permanence of love; there is loss, so there is no decision remorse. Once you experience loss, it is easy for your mind to accept coins, and it is easy for your mind to play duality, for your mind was created for that game, yes? Coins of the right and left hemispheres, conscious and unconscious; right? Flip and I will see the luck of the day, but oh wise one, the Knowledge Seeker you are, and the remembrance of your holy connection being so in tune with you and your beautiful friend, Jack, allowed you to make the right decision, and in doing so, there is no loss. His joy of supporting you through your hardships became your joy in supporting him through his hardships. Together your dance of love allows you and him to be in tune to the divine blueprint of partnership, acknowledging the grace, the courage, the strength, and the honor to share that dance today with him. And yes, your love is enough.

So, there you have it. Raphael so gracefully put into words my joy in loving a little dog named Jack and that part of our Life Purposes was to be a good partnership to help us both through our hard times in an unconditional giving and receiving. There is no guilt in love, and the process of knowing loss allows this love to come through and win the game of duality. It does not make these decisions easier, but what it did for me was give me a way to go to Source and ask for input when deciding what I know deep in my heart was the right one. The peaceful but sad moments at the ending of a life not only bring closure to one story but also open the avenue to a whole new story. Remembering the good times bring a smile and a knowing that Jack and I will once again chase squirrels through the mud and be forever connected in Spirit.

The Three Points

When life is framed within the confines of grief, it can be limiting in choices for the survivor. I think that the rest of the world thinks that choices are easy, or they want that for you as the survivor. My experience tells me otherwise. While grief is different for everyone, there seems to be a commonality in the questions that I hear from people. How do I move forward? How do I survive without my spouse? Why does grief take so long to get over? What does normal look like now? These are just some of the questions that linger after the death of anyone and can keep the strongest of us confined within the framework of that box, trying to punch our way out.

I was there in that box trying to decide if I even wanted to fight my way out. It turns out that at the time, I did not even have the strength to make a hole in the box, and the only thing that I knew was that if I was going to survive, I needed some tools to help me break free.

Looking back, I have determined that I created a method for me that I call the Three Points of Survival. Let me explain what this is.

Body: When my wife died, I needed a way to get my body to not be so exhausted and powerless. At the time, I felt like I was 120 years old, and even though my mind said I should go for a walk around the block, my body said that there is no way that was going to happen as it literally gave anyone viewing me the impression that I was a stooped-over version of a man who seemed to have some disease of the legs, because I sure didn't move more than a few inches at a time. I realized quickly that if I was going to challenge this vision, then I had to set some sort of realistic goal of standing up straight and taking bigger steps. I don't want to give anyone the wrong impression. This took an incredible amount of effort because of the pain both physically and mentally, as well as the time needed to get stronger and walk farther in the day to day challenge of fighting the grief body.

Mind: Getting out from under the mind-deadening afterglow of grief can be debilitating, and in my case, I was always second-guessing the decisions leading up to my wife's death. I had to overcome all the negative thoughts and try to formulate a plan to reach out and touch another way of thinking. Grief has a way of placing you a cathartic state where you can't seem to respond to anyone else's input, let alone yours. But, one event for me was noticed as I watched a movie and saw someone writing a blog. I don't know why that one visual produced a thought that I should write a blog about my journey through grief, but it did, and over time it opened my mind again and ultimately allowed me to think new thoughts and replace the ones that were beating me up. That eventually led to writing a book on the same subject matter and sent me on the journey to grief counselor training. It just proved to me that even when you don't think your mind is registering anything, there are times when things do get through, and even the slightest movement toward new ideas can, in the long run, create movement forward.

Spirit: The definition of *Spirit* to me is any belief system, whether religious or not, where you can connect to a source outside your conditioning.

So, in my weakened state of grief and not necessarily being very responsive to anything, reaching out seemed darned impossible. But what I was willing to do is listen and feel my way back across the stepping-stones, in my mind, being placed in front of me to help guide me back.

As all three of these areas began strengthening over time, the clouds started to lift, I started to notice an improvement in the strength of my body, mind, and spirit. Although there were ups and downs, the important thing to remember is that it is your choice. There is no right or wrong when it comes to grief, and everything is indeed a choice. If you want to move into a new but different way after the loss of someone, then it is possible. If you don't, then that is a choice as well.

Finally, the two things that will help you along the way is too be consistent and persistent. As hard as grief is, making the choice to come out and be a strong survivor is very difficult. You must be consistent enough in your thinking to know that if you just continue on the path you will see improvement. You also must be persistent because nature and that wonderful thing called ego will make it difficult and you will need to stand strong over time.

Of course, your journey is an individualized story of grief, and no system will benefit everyone. But what my journey told me is that by working on all three of the areas, it gave me a chance. The lesson learned is that it is helpful to create a system for yourself that you can live within that gives you a chance to succeed and to overcome grief. Whatever system you develop will be perfect because the most important thing is that you buy into the process and see improvement, even if it is baby steps.

Separation

Separation comes in many shapes and sizes.
between Spouses,
between loves,
between children and hugs.

Separation is not the end.
it allows those involved
to come back again.

They take their energy with them,
add and subtract love,
and bring it back to combine in time,
and restore the oneness.

So, don't be sad to say goodbye.
know in your heart it is only the beginning.
You are never separate when you are
one to begin with.

A Short Walk to Forgiveness

Let me set a scene for you. You arrive home from a soccer game with your nine-year-old son in tow following his game. You are hot and tired from being in the elements, and as you drudge up to the house, your wife comes out and asks where your daughter is. It hits you like a bolt of lightning that you had two kids with you when you went to the game and now only have one. The look of shock on your wife's face says it all. No need to react in any other way but to drive like a bat out of hell to the field. You pull up to the field and what do you find? The field is completely empty. No parents, coaches—or one little girl.

Except wait. There, walking down the street dragging a full-size lawn chair is Betty Grace. It was absolutely the saddest and, at the same time, the happiest thing that I had ever seen. I yelled at her, and in slow motion this strong little girl turned around, and yes, there were tears flowing down her cheek. I did my usual father routine and blamed everything and everyone that I could think of while the same time hugging her and crying myself.

To this day, more than thirty years later, I struggle with this incident. It has been a running family joke all these years: "be careful; Dad might forget you somewhere." I know that I have repeatedly told her I was sorry; of course, I tried to make it up to her as she grew up, and I am sure that I did in some ways and not in others. But I am not sure that I ever asked her to forgive me, which I am doing right now. The thing is that forgiveness must come from me first and go outward. Forgiving myself for something that happened so long ago is really the first step in the bigger picture of forgiveness. If you cannot forgive yourself for something whether trivial or large, then you are always going to hold onto it and let it fester into something that will affect you the rest of your life. We all have forgiveness issues whether it is with family, friends, work, or any other daily things that pop up. Forgiveness releases you from the jail cell you have created yourself one bar at a time by holding onto things that, in the long run, are not important for your movement toward home.

Challenge yourself by looking at your own need to use forgiveness for whatever reason and live without the bars of your self-created prison. Enjoy the freedom and breathe in the fresh air created when you knock those walls down. Forgive, forgive, forgive is what we should all be saying to ourselves as we move into new energy.

Oh, and Betty Grace, I know you forgive me, but now I forgive myself. Love always. Dad

Dropping into Memory

Anniversaries come and go, but some linger like the drops of rain hanging on hummingbird feeder outside. They don't want to let go, so they hang on until the weather changes and dries them up or the force of the wind knocks them from their perch. Anniversaries are important reminders of the past celebrated with the care that should have afforded them. But they become less celebrated after someone leaves us and remind us what we miss and cannot do anything about.

When these days come up for me, I sometimes do not even realize what time of the year it is, and then bam, I get hit upside of the head with a memory that tells me in no uncertain terms that I am to remember something and, oh yeah, pay attention. Then, for me the floodgates open and memories stream in so fast that I have a hard time separating the appropriate pictures swirling throughout my mind, so they become a jumbled mess. You would think that these memories could come in an organized fashion and communicate in a linear way so that I could view them in context. But that is not how memory works.

Sitting at my desk on the ninth anniversary of an event so profound to me that I can't believe the Earth didn't stop turning for even just a second creates a cloud of emotions mixed with pictures. Oh, I realize what day it is now. This event was the day that my wife Barbara died from complications of Diabetes. It is not like we forget intentionally, but life has a way of weaving a cocoon around us that is supposed to protect us from hurt, pain, and anguish. But every year, pretty much exactly as scheduled, my internal time clock sets off an alarm and leads me down the rabbit hole of a life review with someone that I spent so many years with. I want to thank that clock for going off every year because without it, I would be concerned that not using these memories would make them go away forever.

For me, playing in these jumbled memories every year helps me to stay connected to the importance of my life. Even though they are not all fun to relive, they are mine, and I can take them with me on the rest of the journey and mix them up with new memories. So, when it comes to the end of my time here, I can say that I connected. I don't need to be like that waterdrop and hang on. Letting go will bring new memories that I can share in, and thanks to this incredible body, I know that I am going to get hit upside the head occasionally. That is perfect.

The lesson learned is this: do not try to control your memories; allow them to flow from the drips in the direction that they need to go. Being free to sort out the jumbled mess is a job that can be thought of as an honor in remembering the soul that touched your life. Enjoy the reminders.

New Beginnings

During the grief journey, I often wondered if I could obtain a normal life again. Of course, there is a big assumption here: that I had a normal life to begin with. So, considering that we all come from skewed visions of what this normal is, my definition was being married, having kids, working one job my whole life, and rocking in the chair on the porch next to the one I married when I was twenty-one. Okay, it does seem a little Beaver Cleaver now that I say it aloud. But really, "normal" is something that we all come at from different points of view.

My normal question was, Could it be possible giving the harshness of death, grieving, and recovery to expect anything resembling the normal that was in my first life? Obviously, the real answer is no. My naïve and protective shield I was building around myself provided an unrealistic cushion that gave me the hope that would help lead me out of the grayness.

Here is my analysis of this normal. Expecting the normal to continue is perfectly normal, but as you move through the grief process, know that normal will show itself as you progress through your life, meet new people along the way, and find that you are in a new place. None of it is bad, but it will be different. It is all perfectly good, and the new normal will probably surprise you because you never thought that you would survive.

When you are in the trenches, thinking that your life will ever be normal again is hard, but I believe most of us crave this new normal even if it looks different. We don't like to stand out in a crowd, so to speak, and be different or that we just can't seem to get it together based on expectation of society. My real opinion of society is we need to find our new normal on our own time and in our own way and really shouldn't be concerned about everyone else's perception of what normal for us should look like. I am pretty sure you wouldn't wish the grief process on anyone. But the reality is that we all will go through this at one point or another, which makes it almost a learning lesson that you can pass on once you get grounded in your own new normal.

None of this is easy. To rationally think about this in the beginning stages of grief is almost impossible. But slowly, for most people, a point comes into view around that corner that you could not see before. You start thinking differently about that road ahead and have just the slightest twinge of hope that there really could be a normal that you could live with and incorporate into a resemblance of a life. You accept that it will never be the same, but the realization comes that it doesn't have to be the same. You only assumed that your life had to remain the same, but guess what? There are many roads that can be taken to get a person to the same destination.

Why not let it fall into place and allow yourself the moment of taking in a new breath that doesn't require the angst of worrying about how you are going to pull this off. Take that breath and know that whatever road you take will be perfect and will get you to the end, and most importantly there can be more than one destination. Enjoy the new normal as it unfolds and just watch the way your breathing returns to normal.

A More Peaceful Definition

The word *grief* brings the impression of negativity, like when you are supposed to act, feel, or think a certain way. This continues through the timeline that is created by other's thoughts around us that have lost someone. It is almost like grievers are the ones being directed on stage by an unknown force. But my contention is that the phrase "moments of remembrance" would much better explain grief. Think about it—we would no longer be caught in the trap of society's control-conscious, albeit well-intentioned, word *grief.*

Moments of remembrance completely frees us to create the pictures in our head that we need to transverse through the minefields of emotions that always come in over time. Just a little change in semantics gives us all the freedom to move away from the negative side of the word and truly focus on what will lead us down the healing path.

If we stay in the moments of remembrance, society will no longer put us in that box of grief that it feels is its obligation. Instead, it allows all of us to take the course of action that is best for us and in our own timeframe with less interference by ego and the good intenders.

Changing a word seems so easy, but what it really brings you is the freedom to grieve the way you want to. The journey is yours, so if a change in words helps, why not try it? Thinking of these things while you are in the process is hard, so I understand the simple-minded approach to saying this. When we are in the grief process, it is hard not only to function from a physical, mental, and emotional level but also to think of other things to add would be virtually be impossible. In one respect, we want to grief because it is our rite of passage. On the other hand, we don't know how to grieve in a way that would conform to our own morals let alone to the world at large. Coming up with suggestions on the grieving process after the fact is easy. We humans learn well after we have experienced something.

The only helpful suggestion that I can pass on after being through my own grieving events is that I don't want others to suffer as much as I seemed too. If we can pass it on, so to speak, and help others on their own journeys by offering simple ways that might make their journey a little less painful, then I believe any suggestion good.

If a change in wording allows someone to focus on the good memories and it brings comfort to their being by staying away from a negative word like *grief*, then so be it. For me, in times of loss, remembering the moments allowed me to take that step forward and meet another day with the hope that the horizon would bring a day of brighter colors and a new journey.

Boxed In

Boxes are square, in case you didn't know that. They hold things in while at the same time not allowing things to get out. I admit something here that took me a long time to realize: I have created boxes for my family that I thought were important to work within. That sounds easy to say, but from an emotional level, it almost takes me to my knees. I realized with the help of Archangel Raphael, that my whole life has been an act of staying within the boxes created by people, family, society, and the mass consciousness. I always wanted to be the good son, father, and husband, and I was always willing to give in to whatever it took to stay within the boxes of what was proper. Of course, "proper" is defined by—guess who—others. Creating waves was not ever on my radar. Even in my banking career, those boxes were an important part of me moving up the ranks and conforming to the corporate world of rules and regulations.

What I realize now is that my passion dissolved into the background with that conforming behavior and that a lot of years were spent moving away from and not to what was in my heart. This is by no means a bad thing, but the realization that I passed along this box mentality to my children was profoundly unsettling only because I believe now that by not following the passion of your intended journey, you affect the soul's true journey of being here.

We all do this in case you didn't recognize this box dilemma in yourself. Conformity strips us of our purpose and creates, especially for our youth, the idea that they can never live to fulfill their own destiny. I believe that just realizing that the boxes exist and that we are individual souls on our own journeys of passion and destiny will enlighten us. Opening to the impact that we have on our youth just might allow the boxes to tear a little and give them the permission to seek their own destinies no matter how messy it is or how it deviates from the straight line we are judging it from. Our perspective is not important. They are the future of this planet, so let them lead. The boxes we place around our children create a few pressures that sometimes push them to extremes in order to feel that they can or want to conform to our world or rules and regulations. We all have to take responsibility for creating an environment that has contributed in one way or another to their need to find other ways to cope. Helping to remove these societal boxes from our children might help in fixing problems such as self-medicating as we get out of their way and let them live the lives that they came to do.

I am thankful that an Angel opened my eyes to the possibilities outside of the box and just hope that it is not too late to allow new leadership in to fix this boxed-in planet.

Peace

If peace had a feeling,
it would feel like a slight breeze
swirling around the body.
The coolness of the water at the river's edge.
The look of a lover when the time is right.
The warmth of the sun's rays
as they float through the tree,
and gently rest on the arm.
Sitting in a meadow high in the mountains,
listening to nothing
and to everything at the same time.

Peace comes in many flavors,
moments and sounds.
Being aware is only half of it.
Feeling peace is the completion.

Transitions

I would like to talk about death. Of course, talking about death usually means a conversation about the physical death of the body you have grown so close to. But there is another death that, no matter what religious persuasion you might be from or none, you do, at some point, wonder about Spiritual death. You can use all kinds of words about this, but the point is we do wonder, imagine, dream, meditate, and talk about what might be on the other side of the veil, so to speak. I am not pronouncing to be an expert on this, but the more I study and follow my heart, I believe what makes sense for me is that I am choosing to be Spiritually non-dead.

What I mean by being "Spiritually non-dead" is that I do not believe that my Spirit dies. So, how can I ever die except in physical form? I developed this premise over a lifetime of being around and watching members of my family go through physical death. What I have added to that premise is the understanding developed over years of reading books and listening to tapes from sources all over the world about this process. What I have learned and how I determine what is right for me has always been how I felt about the subject. At an early age, I remember thinking that with all the people who die, it had to get way too crowded in Heaven, so it just made sense to me that there had to be some sort of recycling going on. I remember even at five thinking that was a funny thought, but it felt right so I stuck with it.

No matter how you think of death, it does help me, and I am sure others, that there is a plan bigger than what we see. That gives us a structure to hold onto even though we will not know for sure until the door opens. But my point is that it should be okay for people to have a picture in their heads about these expectations. If nothing else, for those going through the process of physical death and those left behind, it provides a more relaxed place to be.

If you know someone who is ill, dying, or even grieving, do not be afraid to talk to them about it. Love has many ways to effect peace. Be part of the peace process as you help people through their journey.

The Ring

Looking down at my left hand and realizing that I had the wedding ring on my finger wasn't really a surprise, but it caught me off guard that I even had an awareness that surpassed the normal day to day survival mode that I had been in. That "normal" at the time was based on my thoughts that I had to continue working hard to care about what I was doing after the death of my first wife. The power of grief can take away a person's motivation and will to do anything. But, when you have a family to take care of, you force yourself to go through the motions of being in this world, but at the same time, you are not there. Where are you?

I believe during grief, you are in the same place that the ring is. You and the ring are there, but you are in the gray fog bank that envelopes everything. There is no right or wrong to this grief stuff, and individually we all act different. When you start to sense and take in the world around you again, you can catch yourself reacting to a ring on your finger.

The ring in my case had been there for over thirty-four years and had created an indentation that, at the time, didn't hardly allow the ring to be turned, let alone come off. But that I noticed it meant to me that I was seeing less of the fog and more of the life that was going on around me. The pain was still very much a part of my daily life, but little things, like the ring, began to populate my mind, where up until then, every minute faded into every other minute; time meant nothing, and numbness was my best friend.

The ring and I had a conversation at one point, and it was decided it was time it came off. This ring had a mind of its own. Soap, grease, and pulling and prodding did nothing to expedite its removal. I felt like it was saying it wasn't time to separate from this beautiful relationship that I remember saying years before that I would die with this ring on.

So I gave in and wore it while waking up to the world again and getting on with my life both in business and family until the time that I wanted to share space with someone new came into my life and felt that the time was right to create a separation from my past life. Having the ring cut off at a jeweler, I thought, would be emotional, but I guess coming back into life allowed me the grace to accept that my moving on was important. The ring came off, leaving a very white and indented presence on my finger.

Time goes by when you enter the real world again, so when the time came to join with another beautiful human being again, the thought of rings came up. Being older, both of us really did not have a need for formalities, so it was suggested that I fix the ring that I have and add a new engraving. Now, this normally would seem to be against the code somehow. But at the time, it just felt like the perfect balance of the past to the future: two people who have been so influential in my life are together on my hand, and we move to whatever is placed in front of us through the rest of life. It is beautiful if you think about it. Combining the love of the past with the love of the future gives me a warmth that I can't explain. No one is left out of the story. I carry all the years that flew by in a little gold ring along with the hope of the future with me, and we get to share this journey together.

Little things like this help all of us to come out of the fog bank when the time is right. By being at peace is part of the journey and, if you can, paying attention to the subtle things happening around you, you just might find a path that will work for you and enter a new world. It worked for me, and I hope you find your ring and how it fits into your new story.

All is Well

*Angels enter the room,
voicing "all is well,"
with chimes in the background,
and stunned silence all around.*

*The ego says,
don't you believe it,
unless there is an epiphany
to bow down too.*

*The heart says,
wouldn't that be lovely.
I feel it so strongly
that you are speaking to me.*

*The mind says,
well, it is about time.
I have been waiting
patiently, now what?*

*The body says,
thank you,
I can finally let go,*

*and not carry the world
on my shoulders.*

*The Angels smile,
and remind the ego, heart,
mind and body, that all they said was,
"all is well."*

*No epiphany required,
no emotions requested,
no process needs to be followed,
and no stresses released.*

*All is well, always.
From the Source,
to the individual cells,
from the beginning to the end.
From the first love,
to the last love.*

*You chose to have faith
that Angels could appear,
and gave you a message
that "all is well."*

Acknowledgments

This book is a continuation of my previous books which centers on developing a spiritual skill set in a stream of daily bombardment that tends to sway us away from awakening. But, what I discovered when I wrote the first book and had no clue how to produce a book let alone writing it, I met people on the journey that filled the gaps of my lack of understanding. Ultimately, these people created a team that guided my thoughts to the eventual outcome of understanding the process, and how to write in a way that sounded like me. That is a challenge in any time period. So, with that understanding comes the knowledge that it really does take a village. My thanks for taking this Soul on and helping me reach beyond myself goes out to my Publisher, Sharon Lund of Sacred Life Publishers, whose gentle encouragement made all the difference. Wendy Jo Dymond edited and made suggestions that continues to make my writing look better.

My family is always an inspiration to me and through our joint experiences provides me with a motivation to say what I feel. I thank them all for loving me enough to let me live in my world without too much interference.

Finally, I would like to thank the friends I have who read my writings and encourage me with their words.

About the Author

Mike Russell

Through a series of events over Mike Russell's life including broadcasting school, journalism in college, and his adventures into the spiritual realm after the death of his wife, he found that he was at a crossroads of discovery that he did not want to turn away from. He took what he had learned over the years while raising a family and working in the financial services industry, and realized the skills that he thought didn't connect did indeed create a bigger set of proficiencies that he could use in a new way. The results were a blog, newsletters, and articles written for the grief community, as well as two previous books, *A Journey of Discovery through Intuition with Help from the Angels*, and *My Compass, Our Story, A Journey through Death and Life*.

Mike's belief that the many random events in one's life truly are not random as they all add up to the congregated form that exits for a reason, and can be creative no matter what age a person is. Artistic expression can be achieved no matter what a person's background and developed skills are, just by connecting the dots on the journey.

Enjoy the journey and know that you are enough.

www.ingramcontent.com/pod-product-compliance
Lightning Source LLC
Chambersburg PA
CBHW071437080526
44587CB00014B/1892